Candide

Crofts Classics

GENERAL EDITORS

Samuel H. Beer, *Harvard University*
O. B. Hardison, Jr., *Georgetown University*

VOLTAIRE

Candide
or
Optimism

EDITED BY

Norman L. Torrey

COLUMBIA UNIVERSITY

Harlan Davidson, Inc.
Arlington Heights, Illinois 60004

LIBRARY OF CONGRESS CATALOGING-IN-PUBLICATION DATA

Voltaire, 1694–1778.
    Candide, or, Optimism.

    (Crofts classics)
    Translation of Candide.
    Bibliography: p.
    I. Torrey, Norman L. (Norman Lewis), 1894–   .
II. Title. III. Title: Candide. IV. Title:
Optimism.
PQ2082.C3E5   1985b   843'.5   85-25343
ISBN 0-88295-100-9 (pbk.)

MANUFACTURED IN THE UNITED STATES OF AMERICA

91   90   49   50   51   EB

Contents

Important Dates in Voltaire's Life

1694   François-Marie Arouet was born in Paris on November 21.

1704-1711   A student at the Jesuit school of Louis-le-Grand.

1711-1716   Years of literary formation. The study of law abandoned.

(1715   Death of Louis XIV. 1715-1723 Regency of Philippe d'Orléans.)

1717-1718   Eleven months in the Bastille for satirical poems that he probably did not write.

1723   Epic poem, *La Henriade*, first published secretly under the name of *La Ligue*, describing the religious wars of the sixteenth century and celebrating the tolerant spirit of Henry IV.

1726   Sent again to the Bastille because of a quarrel with Chevalier de Rohan, a nobleman by birth. Released soon, but forced into exile.

1726-1729   Three years of exile, spent mostly in England, where he learned the language, saw Shakespeare played, and studied English life and letters.

1731   *History of Charles XII, King of Sweden,* the first historical writing in the modern manner.

1732   Produced *Zaïre*, one of his best plays.

1733-1734   Published his witty and philosophical *Letters on the English Nation*.

1734-1749   Years spent in the study of physics, metaphysics and history, in company with the learned Mme. du Châtelet.

1745   At court, as Historiographer of France.

1746   Elected to the French Academy.

1748   *Zadig,* a philosophical tale.

1750   Scorned by Louis XV, Voltaire went hopefully to Berlin to serve as philosopher-poet to Frederick the Great.

1751-1752   Published *The Age of Louis XIV* and *Micromégas*.

1753   Quarreled with Frederick on an issue of right against might.

1754   Unwelcome in France, Voltaire wandered in the border regions looking for a home.

1755-1758   Acquired properties in Lausanne and Geneva, finally settling in a Genevan château, which he called *Les Délices*.

1756   *Poem on Natural Law. Poem on the Lisbon Disaster. Universal History.*

1759   *Candide*. Voltaire moved to Ferney, near Geneva but on French soil, and became a gentleman-farmer.

1762   Undertook the rehabilitation of Calas, who had been cruelly and unjustly executed at Toulouse. Judgment reversed in 1765. The first of a series of campaigns against fanaticism and barbarous judicial procedures.

1763   *Treatise on Tolerance*.

1764   *Dictionnaire philosophique*. Voltaire is now openly hostile to the Church, because of its persecuting power.

1764-1777   The Patriarch of Ferney becomes Europe's greatest champion of humanity.

1778   Returned to Paris, received tremendous ovations. Died there on May 30.

Introduction

In contrast to the witty, bantering, ironical, lightly satiri
cal tone of *Candide,* the subject of this philosophical tale is
the problem of evil. If God is both All-powerful and Good,
whence comes evil into the world? This problem has ob-
sessed man at least since the Biblical Job. An explanation
popular in Voltaire's day was called philosophical optimism, of which the best-known exponents were the German
philosopher, Leibnitz, and the English poet, Pope. It was
based on the belief that God, the perfect Father, created the
universe out of chaos, or imperfection, and in His goodness
created the best of all possible worlds. The existence of evil
was not denied, but it was claimed that every degree of evil
was a necessary link in the Great Chain of Being. As a
whole the universe was good. Man should not only accept
his lot, but should not try to change it. Even particular evil
and individual suffering played an essential role in the total
harmony.

Voltaire never took kindly to this theory. The Lisbon
earthquake of November 1, 1755, compelled him to voice
strenuous objections. It was the direct inspiration, first of a
serious poem on that disaster, and then, three years later, of
Candide. It shook whatever faith he may have had in God's
Providence and also clearly revealed to him the absurdity of
the philosophical explanation. As a reformer he believed
that many evils were avoidable, especially those caused by
ignorance and fanaticism. Philosophical optimism he therefore called "a doctrine of despair under a consoling name,'
because it tolerated evil as necessary in a predestined har-
monious order. It was his conviction that the abstract good
of the whole could have no meaning for the suffering individual and could be of no consolation to him. The unif

ing theme of *Candide* is the reduction to absurdity of that doctrine.

Voltaire's objections to Pope's "clear truth" that "whatever is, is right" and his belief that "God sends not ill, if rightly understood: or partial ill is universal good," are satirically treated throughout the story. But even more ridiculous in Voltaire's eyes was the metaphysical jargon of Leibnitz. His "sufficient reason" (synonymous with "cause"), his "pre-established harmony," posited to explain the parallel functioning, without interaction, of the body and the mind, his outmoded physical notions of monades and the plenum, and above all his repeated references to this best of all possible worlds, are the constant objects of Voltaire's satire.

Voltaire found a way, too, to protest against the worst political and religious abuses of his day: the folly of dynastic wars, the cruelties of the Inquisition, the refusal of the Church to bury actors and actresses, the monastic vows forced by parents upon unwilling younger children, etc., etc. Only in Eldorado, a non-existent utopia, were things really governed for the best.

He does not of course attempt to solve the problem of evil. With Locke, he believed that the solution was beyond the limits of human understanding. Only by a frank acceptance of man's fate, with all its limitations, can life be made endurable. Man should therefore work without theorizing, because "work keeps at bay three great evils: boredom, vice and need." Voltaire's answer is that we should cultivate our gardens. By implication, however, there is no law against uprooting the noxious weeds.

*   *   *   *

In this often reprinted English version, which is essentially that of Richard Aldington, a very few minor changes have been made in the interests of accuracy. The editing was greatly facilitated by the excellent French editions of *Candide* by André Morize and George R. Havens.

Chapter I

HOW CANDIDE WAS BROUGHT UP IN A NOBLE CASTLE AND HOW HE WAS EXPELLED FROM THE SAME

In the castle of Baron Thunder-ten-tronckh in Westphalia [1] there lived a youth, endowed by Nature with the most gentle character. His face was the expression of his soul. His judgment was quite honest and he was extremely simpleminded; and this was the reason, I think, that he was named Candide. Old servants in the house suspected that he was the son of the Baron's sister and a decent honest gentleman of the neighborhood, whom this young lady would never marry because he could only prove seventy-one quarterings,[2] and the rest of his genealogical tree was lost, owing to the injuries of time.

The Baron was one of the most powerful lords in Westphalia, for his castle possessed a door and windows. His Great Hall was even decorated with a piece of tapestry. The dogs in his stable-yards formed a pack of hounds when necessary; his grooms were his huntsmen; the village curate was his Grand Almoner. They all called him "My Lord," and laughed heartily at his stories.

The Baroness weighed about three hundred and fifty pounds, was therefore greatly respected, and did the honors of the house with a dignity which rendered her still more respectable. Her daughter Cunegonde, aged seventeen, was rosy-cheeked, fresh, plump and tempting. The Baron's son

1. **Westphalia** Section of Germany just east of Holland. In Voltaire's day, it was a poor agricultural province through which he passed in 1750 on his way to the court of Frederick the Great.
2. **quarterings** These divisions on coats of arms are indications of the number of noble ancestors.

appeared in every respect worthy of his father. The tutor Pangloss was the oracle of the house, and little Candide followed his lessons with all the candor of his age and character.

Pangloss taught metaphysico-theologo-cosmolonigology.[3] He proved admirably that there is no effect without a cause and that in this best of all possible worlds, My Lord the Baron's castle was the best of castles and his wife the best of all possible Baronesses.

" 'Tis demonstrated," said he, "that things cannot be otherwise; for, since everything is made for an end, everything is necessarily for the best end. Observe that noses were made to wear spectacles; and so we have spectacles. Legs were visibly instituted to be breeched, and we have breeches.[4] Stones were formed to be quarried and to build castles; and My Lord has a very noble castle; the greatest Baron in the province should have the best house; and as pigs were made to be eaten, we eat pork all the year round; consequently, those who have asserted that all is well[5] talk nonsense; they ought to have said that all is for the best."

Candide listened attentively and believed innocently, for he thought Mademoiselle Cunegonde extremely beautiful, although he was never bold enough to tell her so. He decided that after the happiness of being born Baron of Thunder-ten-tronckh, the second degree of happiness was to be Mademoiselle Cunegonde; the third, to see her every day; and the fourth to listen to Doctor Pangloss, the greatest philosopher of the province and therefore of the whole world.

One day when Cunegonde was walking near the castle, in a little wood which was called The Park, she observed Doctor Pangloss in the bushes, giving a lesson in experi-

3. **cosmolonigology** The suggestion is that Pangloss ("all-tongue") is the teacher of abstract nonsense. Swift used a similar term for similar effect in *Gulliver's Travels*.

4. **breeches** Clear but ludicrous examples of what are called in philosophy "final causes," that is, ends or purposes which serve as causes of created things.

5. **all is well** See Introduction for Pope's phrasing.

mental physics to her mother's waiting maid, a very pretty and docile brunette. Mademoiselle Cunegonde had a great inclination for science and watched breathlessly the reiterated experiments she witnessed; she observed clearly the Doctor's sufficient reason, the effects and the causes, and returned home very much excited, pensive, filled with the desire of learning, reflecting that she might be the sufficient reason of young Candide and that he might be hers. 60

On her way back to the castle she met Candide and blushed; Candide also blushed. She bade him good-morning in a hesitating voice; Candide replied without knowing what he was saying. Next day, when they left the table after dinner, Cunegonde and Candide found themselves behind a screen; Cunegonde dropped her handkerchief, Candide picked it up; she innocently held his hand; the young man 70 innocently kissed the young lady's hand with remarkable vivacity, tenderness and grace; their lips met, their eyes sparkled, their knees trembled, their hands wandered. Baron Thunder-ten-tronckh passed near the screen, and, observing this cause and effect, expelled Candide from the castle by kicking him in the backside frequently and hard. Cunegonde swooned; when she recovered her senses, the Baroness slapped her in the face; and all was in consternation in the noblest and most agreeable of all possible castles.

Chapter II

WHAT HAPPENED TO CANDIDE AMONG THE BULGARIANS

Candide, expelled from the earthly paradise, wandered for a long time without knowing where he was going, weeping, turning up his eyes to Heaven, gazing back frequently at the noblest of castles which held the most beautiful of young Baronesses; he lay down to sleep supperless between two furrows in the open fields; it snowed heavily in large flakes. The next morning the shivering Candide, penniless, dying of cold and exhaustion, dragged himself towards the neighboring town, which was called Waldberghoff-trarbk-
10 dikdorff. He halted sadly at the door of an inn. Two men dressed in blue noticed him.

"Comrade," said one, "there's a well-built young man of the right height." They went up to Candide and very civilly invited him to dinner.

"Gentlemen," said Candide with charming modesty, "you do me a great honor, but I have no money to pay my share."

"Ah, sir," said one of the men in blue, "persons of your figure and merit never pay anything; are you not five feet
20 five tall?"

"Yes, gentlemen," said he, bowing, "that is my height."

"Ah, sir, come to table; we will not only pay your expenses, we will never allow a man like you to be short of money; men were only made to help each other."

"You are in the right," said Candide, "that is what Doctor Pangloss was always telling me, and I see that everything is for the best."

They begged him to accept a few crowns, he took them

and wished to give them an I O U; they refused to take it
and all sat down to table. "Do you not love tenderly . . ."   30
"Oh, yes," said he. "I love Mademoiselle Cunegonde ten-
derly."
"No," said one of the gentlemen. "We were asking if you
do not tenderly love the King of the Bulgarians." [1]
"Not a bit," said he, "for I have never seen him."
"What! He is the most charming of Kings, and you must
drink his health."
"Oh, gladly, gentlemen." And he drank.
"That is sufficient," he was told. "You are now the support, the aid, the defender, the hero of the Bulgarians; your   40
fortune is made and your glory assured."
They immediately put irons on his legs and took him to
a regiment.[2] He was made to turn to the right and left,
to raise the ramrod and return the ramrod, to take aim, to
fire, to double up,[3] and he was given thirty strokes with a
stick; the next day he drilled not quite so badly, and received only twenty strokes; the day after, he only had ten,
and was looked on as a prodigy by his comrades.
Candide was completely mystified and could not make
out how he was a hero. One fine spring day he thought he   50
would take a walk, going straight ahead, in the belief that
to use his legs as he pleased was a privilege of the human
species as well as of animals. He had not gone two leagues
when four other heroes, each six feet tall, fell upon him,
bound him and dragged him back to a cell. He was asked
by his judges whether he would rather be thrashed thirty-
six times by the whole regiment or receive a dozen lead bullets at once in his brain. Although he protested that men's
wills are free and that he wanted neither one nor the other,
he had to make a choice; by virtue of that gift of God   60
which is called *liberty,* he determined to run the gauntlet

1. **Bulgarians** Voltaire has his reasons to refer to Frederick the
Great, King of Prussia, under this title.
2. **regiment** It was a common practice in England and on the continent to "press" young men into military service.
3. **double up** Double-time.

thirty-six times and actually did so twice. There were two thousand men in the regiment. That made four thousand strokes which laid bare the muscles and nerves from his neck to his backside. As they were about to proceed to a third turn, Candide, utterly exhausted, begged as a favor that they would be so kind as to smash his head; he obtained this favor; they bound his eyes and he was made to kneel down. At that moment the King of the Bulgarians came by and inquired the victim's crime; and as this King was possessed of a vast genius, he perceived from what he learned about Candide that he was a young metaphysician very ignorant in worldly matters, and therefore pardoned him with a clemency which will be praised in all newspapers and all ages. An honest surgeon healed Candide in three weeks with the ointments recommended by Dioscorides.[4] He had already regained a little skin and could walk when the King of the Bulgarians went to war with the King of the Abares.[5]

4. **Dioscorides** Famous Greek doctor.
5. **Abares** The French-Austrian coalition, which fought against Frederick in the Seven Years' War.

Chapter III

HOW CANDIDE ESCAPED FROM THE BULGARIANS AND WHAT BECAME OF HIM

Nothing could be smarter, more splendid, more brilliant, better drawn up than the two armies. Trumpets, fifes, hautboys, drums, cannons, formed a harmony such as has never been heard even in hell. The cannons first of all laid flat about six thousand men on each side; then the musketry removed from the best of worlds some nine or ten thousand blackguards who infested its surface. The bayonet also was the sufficient reason for the death of some thousands of men. The whole might amount to thirty thousand souls. Candide, who trembled like a philosopher, hid himself as well as he could during this heroic butchery. 10

At last, while the two Kings each commanded a *Te Deum* [1] in his camp, Candide decided to go elsewhere to reason about effects and causes. He clambered over heaps of dead and dying men and reached a neighboring village, which was in ashes; it was an Abare village which the Bulgarians had burned in accordance with international law. Here, old men dazed with blows watched the dying agonies of their murdered wives who clutched their children to their bleeding breasts; there, disembowelled girls who had been made to 20 satisfy the natural appetites of heroes gasped their last sighs; others, half-burned, begged to be put to death. Brains were scattered on the ground among dismembered arms and legs.

Candide fled to another village as fast as he could; it belonged to the Bulgarians, and Abarian heroes had treated it in the same way. Candide, stumbling over quivering limbs

1. **Te Deum** A hymn of thanks to God for victory.

or across ruins, at last escaped from the theatre of war, carrying a little food in his knapsack, and never forgetting Mademoiselle Cunegonde. His provisions were all gone when 30 he reached Holland; but, having heard that everyone in that country was rich and a Christian, he had no doubt at all but that he would be as well treated as he had been in the Baron's castle before he had been expelled on account of Mademoiselle Cunegonde's pretty eyes.

He asked an alms of several grave persons, who all replied that if he continued in that way he would be shut up in a house of correction to teach him how to live. He then addressed himself to a man who had been discoursing on charity in a large assembly for an hour on end. This orator, 40 glancing at him askance, said: "What are you doing here? Are you for the good cause?"

"There is no effect without a cause," said Candide modestly. "Everything is necessarily linked up and arranged for the best. It was necessary that I should be expelled from the company of Mademoiselle Cunegonde, that I ran the gauntlet, and that I beg my bread until I can earn it; all this could not have happened differently."

"My friend," said the orator, "do you believe that the Pope is Anti-Christ?"

50 "I had never heard so before," said Candide, "but whether he is or isn't, I am starving."

"You don't deserve to eat," said the other. "Hence, rascal; hence, you wretch; and never come near me again."

The orator's wife thrust her head out of the window and seeing a man who did not believe that the Pope was Anti-Christ, she poured on his head a full . . . O Heavens! To what excess religious zeal is carried by ladies!

A man who had not been baptized, an honest Anabaptist [2] named Jacques, saw the cruel and ignominious treat-60 ment of one of his brothers, a featherless two-legged creature with a soul; he took him home, cleaned him up, gave him bread and beer, presented him with two florins, and even

2. **Anabaptist** Member of a Protestant sect which opposed infant baptism.

offered to teach him to work at the manufacture of Persian stuffs which are made in Holland. Candide threw himself at the man's feet, exclaiming: "Doctor Pangloss was right in telling me that all is for the best in this world, for I am vastly more touched by your extreme generosity than by the harshness of the gentleman in the black cloak and his good lady."

The next day when he walked out he met a beggar covered with sores, dull-eyed, with the end of his nose fallen away, his mouth awry, his teeth black, who talked huskily, was tormented with a violent cough and spat out a tooth at every cough. 70

Chapter IV

HOW CANDIDE MET HIS OLD MASTER IN PHILOSOPHY, DOCTOR PANGLOSS, AND WHAT HAPPENED

Candide, moved even more by compassion than by horror, gave this horrible beggar the two florins he had received from the honest Anabaptist, Jacques. The phantom gazed fixedly at him, shed tears and threw its arms round his neck. Candide recoiled in terror.

"Alas!" said the wretch to the other wretch, "don't you recognise your dear Pangloss?"

"What do I hear? You, my dear master! You, in this horrible state! What misfortune has happened to you? Why
10 are you no longer in the noblest of castles? What has become of Mademoiselle Cunegonde, the pearl of young ladies, the masterpiece of Nature?"

"I am exhausted," said Pangloss. Candide immediately took him to the Anabaptist's stable where he gave him a little bread to eat; and when Pangloss had recovered: "Well!" said he, "Cunegonde?"

"Dead," replied the other.

At this word Candide swooned; his friend restored him to his senses with a little bad vinegar which happened to be
20 in the stable. Candide opened his eyes. "Cunegonde dead! Ah! best of worlds, where are you? But what illness did she die of? Was it because she saw me kicked out of her father's noble castle?"

"No," said Pangloss. "She was disembowelled by Bulgarian soldiers, after having been raped to the limit of possibility; they broke the Baron's head when he tried to defend her; the Baroness was cut to pieces; my poor pupil was treated exactly like his sister; and as to the castle, there is not one stone standing on another, not a barn, not a sheep, not a duck, not a tree; but we were well avenged, for the 30 Abares did exactly the same to a neighboring barony which belonged to a Bulgarian Lord." At this, Candide swooned again; but, having recovered and having said all that he ought to say, he inquired the cause and effect, the sufficient reason which had reduced Pangloss to so piteous a state.

"Alas!" said Pangloss, " 'tis love; love, the consoler of the human race, the preserver of the universe, the soul of all tender creatures, gentle love."

"Alas!" said Candide, "I am acquainted with this love, this sovereign of hearts, this soul of our soul; it has never 40 brought me anything but one kiss and twenty kicks in the backside. How could this beautiful cause produce in you so abominable an effect?"

Pangloss replied as follows: "My dear Candide! You remember Paquette, the maidservant of our august Baroness; in her arms I enjoyed the delights of Paradise which have produced the tortures of Hell by which you see I am devoured; she was infected and perhaps is dead. Paquette received this present from a most learned monk, who had it from the source; for he received it from an old countess, 50 who had it from a cavalry captain, who owed it to a marchioness, who derived it from a page, who had received it from a Jesuit, who, when a novice, had it in a direct line from one of the companions of Christopher Columbus. For my part, I shall not give it to anyone, for I am dying."

"O Pangloss!" exclaimed Candide, "this is a strange genealogy! Wasn't the devil at the root of it?"

"Not at all," replied that great man. "It was something indispensable in this best of worlds, a necessary ingredient; for, if Columbus in an island of America had not caught 60 this disease, which poisons the source of generation, and often indeed prevents generation, we should not have chocolate and cochineal; [1] it must also be noticed that hitherto in

1. cochineal A scarlet dye, prized in Europe, but an absurdly disproportionate advantage.

our continent this disease is peculiar to us, like theological disputes. The Turks, the Indians, the Persians, the Chinese, the Siamese and the Japanese are not yet familiar with it; but there is a sufficient reason why they in their turn should become familiar with it in a few centuries. Meanwhile, it has made marvellous progress among us, and especially in
70 those large armies composed of honest, well-bred stipendiaries who decide the destiny of States; it may be asserted that when thirty thousand men fight a pitched battle against an equal number of troops, there are about twenty thousand with the pox on either side."

"Admirable!" said Candide. "But you must get cured."

"How can I?" said Pangloss. "I haven't a sou, my friend, and in the whole extent of this globe, you cannot be bled or receive an enema without paying or without someone paying for you."

80   This last speech determined Candide; he went and threw himself at the feet of his charitable Anabaptist, Jacques, and drew so touching a picture of the state to which his friend was reduced that the good easy man did not hesitate to succor Pangloss; he had him cured at his own expense. In this cure Pangloss only lost one eye and one ear. He could write well and knew arithmetic perfectly. The Anabaptist made him his bookkeeper. At the end of two months he was compelled to go to Lisbon on business and took his two philosophers on the boat with him. Pangloss explained to him how
90 everything was for the best. Jacques was not of this opinion.

"Men," said he, "must have corrupted nature a little, for they were not born wolves, and they have become wolves.[2] God did not give them twenty-four-pounder cannons or bayonets, and they have made bayonets and cannons to destroy each other. I might bring bankruptcies into the account and Justice which seizes the goods of bankrupts in order to deprive the creditors of them."

"It was all indispensable," replied the one-eyed doctor, "and private misfortunes make the public good, so that the

2. wolves A favorite contention of Jean-Jacques Rousseau, Voltaire's contemporary.

more private misfortunes there are, the more everything is 100 well." [3]

While he was reasoning, the air grew dark, the winds blew from the four quarters of the globe and the ship was attacked by the most horrible tempest in sight of the port of Lisbon.

3. **well** A further step in reducing philosophical optimism to absurdity.

Chapter V

STORM, SHIPWRECK, EARTHQUAKE,
AND WHAT HAPPENED TO DR.
PANGLOSS, TO CANDIDE AND
THE ANABAPTIST JACQUES

Half the enfeebled passengers, suffering from that inconceivable anguish which the rolling of a ship causes in the
nerves and in all the humors of bodies shaken in contrary
directions, did not retain strength enough even to trouble
about the danger. The other half screamed and prayed; the
sails were torn, the masts broken, the vessel leaking. Those
worked who could, no one cooperated, no one commanded.
The Anabaptist tried to help the crew a little; he was on
the main deck; a furious sailor struck him violently and
10 stretched him on the deck; but the blow he delivered gave
him so violent a shock that he fell head-first out of the ship.
He remained hanging and clinging to part of the broken
mast. The good Jacques ran to his aid, helped him to climb
back, and from the effort he made was flung into the sea in
full view of the sailor, who allowed him to drown without
condescending even to look at him. Candide came up, saw
his benefactor reappear for a moment and then be engulfed
for ever. He tried to throw himself after him into the sea;
he was prevented by the philosopher Pangloss, who proved
20 to him that the Lisbon roads[1] had been expressly created
for the Anabaptist to be drowned in them. While he was
proving this *a priori*,[2] the vessel sank, and every one perished except Pangloss, Candide and the brutal sailor who
had drowned the virtuous Anabaptist; the blackguard swam

1. roads "Where ships may safely ride at anchor."
2. a priori The deductive method of argument which proceeds from
preestablished principles, rather than from experience.

14

successfully to the shore and Pangloss and Candide were carried there on a plank.

When they had recovered a little, they walked toward Lisbon; they had a little money by the help of which they hoped to be saved from hunger after having escaped the storm. Weeping the death of their benefactor, they had 30 scarcely set foot in the town when they felt the earth tremble under their feet; the sea rose in foaming masses in the port and smashed the ships which rode at anchor. Whirlwinds of flame and ashes covered the streets and squares; the houses collapsed, the roofs were thrown upon the foundations, and the foundations were scattered; thirty thousand inhabitants of every age and both sexes were crushed under the ruins. Whistling and swearing, the sailor said: "There'll be something to pick up here."

"What can be the sufficient reason for this phenomenon?" 40 said Pangloss.

"It is the last day!" [3] cried Candide.

The sailor immediately ran among the debris, dared death to find money, found it, seized it, got drunk, and having slept off his wine, purchased the favors of the first woman of good will he met on the ruins of the houses and among the dead and dying. Pangloss, however, pulled him by the sleeve. "My friend," said he, "this is not well, you are disregarding universal reason, you choose the wrong time."

"Blood and 'ounds!" he retorted, "I am a sailor and I was 50 born in Batavia; four times have I stamped on the crucifix during four voyages to Japan; [4] you have found the right man for your universal reason!"

Candide had been hurt by some falling stones; he lay in the street covered with debris. He said to Pangloss: "Alas! Get me a little wine and oil; I am dying."

"This earthquake is not a new thing," replied Pangloss. "The town of Lima felt the same shocks in America last year; similar causes produce similar effects; there must cer-

3. **last day** I.e., the Day of Judgment.
4. **Japan** A regulation imposed on merchants in an attempt to prevent commerce with Christians.

60 tainly be a train of sulphur underground from Lima to Lisbon."

"Nothing is more probable," replied Candide; "but, for God's sake, a little oil and wine."

"What do you mean, probable?" replied the philosopher; "I maintain that it is proved."

Candide lost consciousness, and Pangloss brought him a little water from a neighboring fountain.

Next day they found a little food as they wandered among the ruins and regained a little strength. Afterwards
70 they worked like others to help the inhabitants who had escaped death. Some citizens they had assisted gave them as good a dinner as could be expected in such a disaster; true, it was a dreary meal; the hosts watered their bread with their tears, but Pangloss consoled them by assuring them that things could not be otherwise. "For," said he, "all this is for the best; for, if there is a volcano at Lisbon, it cannot be anywhere else; for it is impossible that things should not be where they are; for all is well."

A little, dark man, a familiar of the Inquisition,[5] who sat
80 beside him, politely took up the conversation, and said: "Apparently, you do not believe in original sin; for, if everything is for the best, there was neither fall nor punishment."[6]

"I most humbly beg your excellency's pardon," replied Pangloss still more politely, "for the fall of man and the curse necessarily entered into the best of all possible worlds."

"Then you do not believe in free will?" said the familiar.

"Your excellency will pardon me," said Pangloss; "free will can exist with absolute necessity; for it was necessary
90 that we should be free; for in short, limited will . . ."

Pangloss was in the middle of his phrase when the familiar nodded to his armed attendant who was pouring out port or Oporto wine for him.

5. **Inquisition** An officer of the Inquisition, or Holy Office, a tribunal which, from the thirteenth century to the eighteenth, attempted to stamp out heresy.

6. **punishment** The fall of man (*Genesis,* iii), with his subsequent redemption, is the orthodox Christian explanation of evil.

Chapter VI

HOW A SPLENDID AUTO-DA-FÉ WAS HELD TO PREVENT EARTHQUAKES, AND HOW CANDIDE WAS FLOGGED

After the earthquake which destroyed three-quarters of Lisbon, the wise men of that country could discover no more efficacious way of preventing a total ruin than by giving the people a splendid *auto-da-fé*.[1] It was decided by the university of Coimbre [2] that the sight of several persons being slowly burned in great ceremony is an infallible secret for preventing earthquakes. Consequently they had arrested a Biscayan convicted of having married his fellow-godmother, and two Portuguese who, when eating a chicken, had thrown away the bacon; [3] after dinner they came and bound Dr. Pangloss and his disciple Candide, one because he had spoken and the other because he had listened with an air of approbation; they were both carried separately to extremely cool apartments,[4] where there was never any discomfort from the sun; a week afterwards each was dressed in a sanbenito [5] and their heads were ornamented with paper mitres; Candide's mitre and sanbenito were painted with flames upside down and with devils who had neither tails nor claws; but Pangloss's devils had claws and tails, and his flames were upright.

Dressed in this manner they marched in procession and

1. **auto-da-fé** "Act of faith"—the ceremony of burning heretics at the stake.
2. **Coimbre** Portuguese city north of Lisbon.
3. **bacon** Thus indicating that they were Jews.
4. **apartments** Ironical for "dank cells."
5. **sanbenito** Ceremonial frocks worn by condemned heretics. Voltaire's description is accurate.

17

listened to a most pathetic sermon, followed by lovely plain song music. Candide was flogged in time to the music, while the singing went on; the Biscayan and the two men who had not wanted to eat the bacon were burned, and Pangloss was hanged, although this is not the custom. The very same day, the earth shook again with a terrible clamor.

Candide, terrified, dumbfounded, bewildered, covered with blood, quivering from head to foot, said to himself: "If this is the best of all possible worlds, what are the others? Let it pass that I was flogged, for I was flogged by the Bulgarians, but, O my dear Pangloss! The greatest of philosophers! Must I see you hanged without knowing why! O my dear Anabaptist! The best of men! Was it necessary that you should be drowned in port! O Mademoiselle Cunegonde! The pearl of women! Was it necessary that your belly should be slit!"

He was returning, scarcely able to support himself, preached at, flogged, absolved and blessed, when an old woman accosted him and said: "Courage, my son, follow me."

Chapter VII

HOW AN OLD WOMAN TOOK CARE OF
CANDIDE AND HOW HE REGAINED
THAT WHICH HE LOVED

Candide did not take courage, but he followed the old woman to a hovel; she gave him a pot of ointment to rub on, and left him food and drink; she pointed out a fairly clean bed; near the bed there was a suit of clothes. "Eat, drink, sleep," said she, "and may our Lady of Atocha, my Lord Saint Anthony of Padua and my Lord Saint James of Compostella take care of you; I shall come back tomorrow."

Candide, still amazed by all he had seen, by all he had suffered, and still more by the old woman's charity, tried to kiss her hand. " 'Tis not my hand you should kiss," said the old woman, "I shall come back tomorrow. Rub on the ointment, eat and sleep."

In spite of all his misfortune, Candide ate and went to sleep. Next day the old woman brought him breakfast, examined his back and smeared him with another ointment; later she brought him dinner, and returned in the evening with supper. The next day she went through the same ceremony.

"Who are you?" Candide kept asking her. "Who has inspired you with so much kindness? How can I thank you?"

The good woman never made any reply; she returned in the evening without any supper. "Come with me," said she, "and do not speak a word."

She took him by the arm and walked into the country with him for about a quarter of a mile; they came to an isolated house, surrounded with gardens and canals. The old woman knocked at a little door. It was opened; she led

Candide up a back stairway into a gilded apartment, left
him on a brocaded sofa, shut the door and went away. Can-
30 dide thought he was dreaming, and felt that his whole life
was a bad dream and the present moment an agreeable
dream. The old woman soon reappeared; she was supporting with some difficulty a trembling woman of majestic
stature, glittering with precious stones and covered with a
veil.

"Remove the veil," said the old woman to Candide. The
young man advanced and lifted the veil with a timid hand.
What a moment! What a surprise! He thought he saw
Mademoiselle Cunegonde, in fact he was looking at her,
40 it was she herself. His strength failed him, he could not utter a word and fell at her feet. Cunegonde fell on the sofa.[1]
The old woman dosed them with distilled waters; they recovered their senses and began to speak: at first they uttered
only broken words, questions and answers at cross purposes,
sighs, tears, exclamations. The old woman advised them to
make less noise and left them alone.

"What! Is it you?" said Candide. "You are alive, and I
find you here in Portugal! Then you were not raped? Your
belly was not slit, as the philosopher Pangloss assured me?"
50 "Yes, indeed," said the fair Cunegonde; "but those two
accidents are not always fatal."

"But your father and mother were killed?"

" 'Tis only too true," said Cunegonde, weeping.

"And your brother?"

"My brother was killed too."

"And why are you in Portugal? And how did you know
I was here? And by what strange adventure have you
brought me to this house?"

"I will tell you everything," replied the lady, "but first of
60 all you must tell me everything that has happened to you
since the innocent kiss you gave me and the kicks you received."

Candide obeyed with profound respect; and, although he

1. **sofa** Ladylike! Voltaire both uses and parodies the recognition
scenes so frequent in tall tales of adventure.

was bewildered, although his voice was weak and trembling, although his back was still a little painful, he related in the most natural manner all he had endured since the moment of their separation. Cunegonde raised her eyes to heaven; she shed tears at the death of the good Anabaptist and Pangloss, after which she spoke as follows to Candide, who did not miss a word and devoured her with his eyes. 70

Chapter VIII

CUNEGONDE'S STORY

"I was fast asleep in bed when it pleased Heaven to send the Bulgarians to our noble castle of Thunder-ten-tronckh; they murdered my father and brother and cut my mother to pieces. A large Bulgarian six feet tall, seeing that I had swooned at the spectacle, began to rape me; this brought me to, I recovered my senses, I screamed, I struggled, I bit, I scratched, I tried to tear out the big Bulgarian's eyes, not knowing that what was happening in my father's castle was a matter of custom; the brute stabbed me with a knife in
10 the left side where I still have the scar."

"Alas! I hope I shall see it," said the naïf Candide.

"You shall see it," said Cunegonde, "but let me go on."

"Go on," said Candide.

She took up the thread of her story as follows: "A Bulgarian captain came in, saw me covered with blood, and the soldier did not disturb himself. The captain was angry at the brute's lack of respect to him, and killed him on my body. Afterwards, he had me bandaged and took me to his billet as a prisoner of war. I washed the few shirts he
20 had and did the cooking; I must admit he thought me very pretty; and I will not deny that he was very well built and that his skin was white and soft; otherwise he had little wit and little philosophy; it was plain that he had not been brought up by Dr. Pangloss. At the end of three months he lost all his money and got tired of me; he sold me to a Jew named Don Issachar, who traded in Holland and Portugal and had a passion for women. This Jew devoted himself to my person but he could not triumph over it; I resisted him better than the Bulgarian soldier; a lady of honor may be

22

raped once, but it strengthens her virtue. In order to sub- 30
due me, the Jew brought me to this country house. Up till
then I believed that there was nothing on earth so splendid
as the castle of Thunder-ten-tronckh; I was undeceived.

"One day the Grand Inquisitor noticed me at Mass; he
ogled me continually and sent a message that he wished to
speak to me on secret affairs. I was taken to his palace; I
informed him of my birth; he pointed out how much it was
beneath my rank to belong to an Israelite. A proposition
was made on his behalf to Don Issachar to give me up to
His Lordship. Don Issachar, who is the court banker and 40
a man of influence, would not agree. The Inquisitor threat-
ened him with an *auto-da-fé*. At last the Jew was frightened
and made a bargain whereby the house and I belong to
both in common. The Jew has Mondays, Wednesdays and
the Sabbath day, and the Inquisitor has the other days of
the week. This arrangement has lasted for six months. It
has not been without quarrels; for it has often been debated
whether the night between Saturday and Sunday belonged
to the old law or the new. For my part, I have hitherto resisted them both; and I think that is the reason why they 50
still love me.

"At last My Lord the Inquisitor was pleased to arrange
an *auto-da-fé* to remove the scourge of earthquakes and to
intimidate Don Issachar. He honored me with an invitation.
I had an excellent seat; and refreshments were served to
the ladies between the Mass and the execution. I was indeed
horror stricken when I saw the burning of the two Jews and
the honest Biscayan who had married his fellow-godmother;
but what was my surprise, my terror, my anguish, when I
saw in a sanbenito and under a mitre a face which resem- 60
bled Pangloss's! I rubbed my eyes, I looked carefully, I
saw him hanged; and I fainted. I had scarcely recovered
my senses when I saw you stripped naked; that was the
height of horror, of consternation, of grief and despair. I
will frankly tell you that your skin is even whiter and of a
more perfect tint than that of my Bulgarian captain. This
spectacle redoubled all the feelings which crushed and de-

voured me. I exclaimed, I tried to say: 'Stop, Barbarians!'
but my voice failed and my cries would have been useless.
70 When you had been well flogged, I said to myself: 'How
does it happen that the charming Candide and the wise
Pangloss are in Lisbon, the one to receive a hundred lashes,
and the other to be hanged, by order of My Lord the Inquisitor, whose darling I am? Pangloss deceived me cruelly
when he said that all is for the best in the world.'

"I was agitated, distracted, sometimes beside myself and
sometimes ready to die of faintness, and my head was filled
with the massacre of my father, of my mother, of my
brother, the insolence of my horrid Bulgarian soldier, the
80 gash he gave me, my slavery, my life as a kitchen wench,
my Bulgarian captain, my horrid Don Issachar, my abominable Inquisitor, the hanging of Dr. Pangloss, that long
plain song *miserere*[1] during which you were flogged, and
above all the kiss I gave you behind the screen that day
when I saw you for the last time. I praised God for bringing
you back to me through so many trials, I ordered my old
woman to take care of you and to bring you here as soon
as she could. She has carried out my commission very well;
I have enjoyed the inexpressible pleasure of seeing you
90 again, of listening to you, and of speaking to you. You must
be very hungry; I have a good appetite; let us begin by
having supper."

Both sat down to supper; and after supper they returned
to the handsome sofa we have already mentioned; they were
still there when Signor Don Issachar, one of the masters of
of the house, arrived. It was the day of the Sabbath. He
came to enjoy his rights and to express his tender love.

1. *miserere* The Latin chant: "Have mercy upon me, O God."

Chapter IX

WHAT HAPPENED TO CUNEGONDE, TO CANDIDE, TO THE GRAND INQUISITOR AND TO A JEW

This Issachar was the most choleric Hebrew who had been seen in Israel since the Babylonian captivity.[1] "What!" said he. "Bitch of a Galilean, isn't it enough to have the Inquisitor? Must this scoundrel share with me too?"

So saying, he drew a long dagger which he always carried and, thinking that his adversary was unarmed, threw himself upon Candide; but our good Westphalian had received an excellent sword from the old woman along with his suit of clothes. He drew his sword, and although he had a most gentle character, laid the Israelite stone-dead on the floor at the feet of the fair Cunegonde.

"Holy Virgin!" she exclaimed, "what will become of us? A man killed in my house! If the police come we are lost."

"If Pangloss had not been hanged," said Candide, "he would have given us good advice in this extremity, for he was a great philosopher. In default of him, let us consult the old woman."

She was extremely prudent and was beginning to give her advice when another little door opened. It was an hour after midnight, and Sunday was beginning. This day belonged to My Lord the Inquisitor. He came in and saw the flogged Candide sword in hand, a corpse lying on the ground, Cunegonde in terror, and the old woman giving advice. At this moment, here is what happened in Candide's soul and the manner of his reasoning: "If this holy man

1. captivity The Jews were held in captivity by the Babylonians in the sixth century, B.C.

calls for help, he will infallibly have me burned; he might do as much to Cunegonde; he had me pitilessly lashed; he is my rival; I am in the mood to kill, there is no room for hesitation."

30   His reasoning was clear and swift; and, without giving the Inquisitor time to recover from his surprise, he pierced him through and through and cast him beside the Jew.

"Here's another," said Cunegonde, "there is no chance of mercy; we are excommunicated, our last hour has come. How does it happen that you, who were born so mild, should kill a Jew and a prelate in two minutes?"

"My dear young lady," replied Candide, "when a man is in love, jealous, and has been flogged by the Inquisition, he is beside himself."

40   The old woman than spoke up and said: "In the stable are three Andalusian horses, with their saddles and bridles; let the brave Candide prepare them; mademoiselle has moidores [2] and diamonds; let us mount quickly, although I can only sit on one buttock, and go to Cadiz; the weather is beautifully fine, and it is most pleasant to travel in the coolness of the night."

Candide immediately saddled the three horses. Cunegonde, the old woman and he rode thirty miles without stopping. While they were riding away, the Holy Her-
50   mandad [3] arrived at the house; My Lord was buried in a splendid church and Issachar was thrown into a sewer.

Candide, Cunegonde and the old woman had already reached the little town of Avacena in the midst of the mountains of the Sierra Morena; and they talked in their inn as follows.

2. moidores Portuguese coin. As a slight concession to local color and realism, Voltaire invariably used the terms for money and food that were proper to the country concerned.

3. Hermandad Holy Brotherhood, an association formed in Spain to track down criminals.

Chapter X

HOW CANDIDE, CUNEGONDE AND THE OLD WOMAN ARRIVED AT CADIZ IN GREAT DISTRESS, AND HOW THEY EMBARKED

"Who can have stolen my pistoles [1] and my diamonds?" said Cunegonde, weeping. "How shall we live? What shall we do? Where shall we find Inquisitors and Jews to give me others?"

"Alas!" said the old woman, "I strongly suspect a reverend Franciscan father who slept in the same inn at Badajoz with us; Heaven forbid that I should judge rashly! But he twice came into our room and left long before we did."

"Alas!" said Candide, "the good Pangloss often proved to me that this world's goods are common to all men and 10 that every one has an equal right to them. According to these principles the monk should have left us enough to continue our journey. Have you nothing left then, my fair Cunegonde?"

"Not a maravedi," [2] said she. "What are we to do?" said Candide.

"Sell one of the horses," said the old woman. "I will ride postillion behind Mademoiselle Cunegonde, although I can only sit on one buttock, and we will get to Cadiz."

In the same hotel there was a Benedictine prior. He 20 bought the horse very cheap.[3] Candide, Cunegonde and the old woman passed through Lucena, Chillas, Lebrixa, and at

1. **pistoles** Spanish gold coin.
2. **maravedi** Copper coin of little value.
3. **cheap** Sudden change in point of view, for ironic effect.

last reached Cadiz.[4] A fleet was there being equipped and troops were being raised to bring to reason the reverend Jesuit fathers of Paraguay,[5] who were accused of causing the revolt of one of their tribes against the kings of Spain and Portugal near the town of Sacramento. Candide, having served with the Bulgarians, went through the Bulgarian drill before the general of the little army with so much
30 grace, celerity, skill, pride and agility,[6] that he was given the command of an infantry company. He was now a captain; he embarked with Mademoiselle Cunegonde, the old woman, two servants, and the two Andalusian horses which had belonged to the Grand Inquisitor of Portugal.

During the voyage they had many discussions about the philosophy of poor Pangloss. "We are going to a new world," said Candide, "and no doubt it is there that everything is for the best; for it must be admitted that one might lament a little over the physical and moral happenings in
40 our own world."

"I love you with all my heart," said Cunegonde, "but my soul is still shocked by what I have seen and undergone."

"All will be well," replied Candide; "the sea in this new world already is better than the seas of our Europe; it is calmer and the winds are more constant. It is certainly the new world which is the best of all possible worlds."

"God grant it!" said Cunegonde, "but I have been so horribly unhappy in mine that my heart is nearly closed to hope."

50 "You complain," said the old woman to them. "Alas! you have not endured such misfortunes as mine."

Cunegonde almost laughed and thought it most amusing of the old woman to assert that she was more unfortunate. "Alas! my dear," said she, "unless you have been raped by two Bulgarians, stabbed twice in the belly, have had two castles destroyed, two fathers and mothers murdered before

4. **Cadiz** Seaport in southern Spain.
5. **Paraguay** This was no imaginary event. Voltaire had a financial interest in one of the ships, the *Pascal*.
6. **agility** The Prussian disciplinary drill was notoriously thorough.

your eyes, and have seen two of your lovers flogged in an *auto-da-fé*, I do not see how you can surpass me; moreover, I was born a Baroness with seventy-two quarterings and I have been a kitchen wench."

50

"You do not know my birth," said the old woman, "and if I showed you my backside you would not talk as you do and you would suspend your judgment."

This speech aroused intense curiosity in the minds of Cunegonde and Candide. And the old woman spoke as follows.

Chapter XI

THE OLD WOMAN'S STORY

"My eyes were not always bloodshot and red-rimmed; my nose did not always touch my chin and I was not always a servant. I am the daughter of Pope Urban X[1] and the Princess of Palestrina. Until I was fourteen I was brought up in a palace to which all the castles of your German Barons would not have served as stables; and one of my dresses cost more than all the magnificence of Westphalia. I increased in beauty, in grace, in talents, among pleasures, respect and hopes; already I inspired love, my breasts were
10 forming; and what breasts! White, firm, carved like those of the Venus de' Medici. And what eyes! What eyelids! What black eyebrows! What fire shone from my two eyeballs, and dimmed the glitter of the stars, as the local poets pointed out to me. The women who dressed and undressed me fell into ecstasy when they beheld me in front and behind; and all the men would have liked to be in their place.

"I was betrothed to a ruling prince of Massa-Carrara. What a prince! As beautiful as I was, formed of gentleness and charms, brilliantly witty and burning with love; I
20 loved him with a first love, idolatrously and extravagantly. The marriage ceremonies were arranged with unheard of pomp and magnificence; there were continual fêtes, revels and comic operas; all Italy wrote sonnets for me and not a good one among them.

"I touched the moment of my happiness when an old marchioness who had been my prince's mistress invited him to take chocolate with her; less than two hours afterwards he

1. **Urban X** In a note Voltaire remarked on "the author's" delicacy, there never having been a pope by this name.

died in horrible convulsions; but that is only a trifle. My mother was in despair, though less distressed than I, and wished to absent herself for a time from a place so disas- 30 trous. She had a most beautiful estate near Gaeta; [2] we embarked on a galley, gilded like the altar of St. Peter's at Rome. A Salle [3] pirate swooped down and boarded us; our soldiers defended us like soldiers of the Pope; they threw down their arms, fell on their knees and asked the pirates for absolution *in articulo mortis.*[4]

"They were immediately stripped as naked as monkeys and my mother, our ladies of honor and myself as well. The diligence with which these gentlemen strip people is truly admirable; but I was still more surprised by their in- 40 serting a finger in a place belonging to all of us where we women usually only allow the end of a syringe. This appeared to me a very strange ceremony; but that is how we judge everything when we leave our own country. I soon learned that it was to find out if we had hidden any diamonds there; 'tis a custom established from time immemorial among the civilised nations who roam the seas. I have learned that the religious Knights of Malta [5] never fail in it when they capture Turks and Turkish women; this is an international law which has never been broken. 50

"I will not tell you how hard it is for a young princess to be taken with her mother as a slave to Morocco; you will also guess all we had to endure in the pirates' ship. My mother was still very beautiful; our ladies of honor, even our waiting maids possessed more charms than could be found in all Africa; and I was ravishing, I was beauty, grace itself, and I was a virgin; I did not remain so long; the flower which had been reserved for the handsome prince of Massa-Carrara was ravished from me by a pirate captain; he was an abominable negro who thought he was 60

2. **Gaeta** Italian port north of Naples.
3. **Salle** A Moroccan port for pirates.
4. **mortis** Being at the point of death.
5. **Malta** Old religious and military order, which dated from the Crusades.

doing me a great honor. The Princess of Palestrina and I must indeed have been strong to bear up against all we endured before our arrival in Morocco! But let that pass; these things are so common that they are not worth mentioning.

"Morroco was swimming in blood when we arrived. The fifty sons of the Emperor Muley Ismael had each a faction; and this produced fifty civil wars, of blacks against blacks, browns against browns, mulattoes against mulattoes. There was continual carnage throughout the whole extent of the empire.

Scarcely had we landed when blacks of a party hostile to that of my pirate arrived with the purpose of depriving him of his booty. After the diamonds and the gold, we were the most valuable possessions. I witnessed a fight such as is never seen in your European climates. The blood of the northern peoples is not sufficiently ardent; their madness for women does not reach the point which is common in Africa. The Europeans seem to have milk in their veins; but vitriol and fire flow in the veins of the inhabitants of Mount Atlas and the neighboring countries. They fought with the fury of the lions, tigers and serpents of the country to determine who should have us. A Moor grasped my mother by the right arm, my captain's lieutenant held her by the left arm; a Moorish soldier held one leg and one of our pirates seized the other. In a moment nearly all our women were seized in the same way by four soldiers. My captain kept me hidden behind him; he had a scimitar in his hand and killed everybody who opposed his fury. I saw my mother and all our Italian women torn in pieces, gashed, massacred by the monsters who disputed them. The prisoners, my companions, those who had captured them, soldiers, sailors, blacks, browns, whites, mulattoes and finally my captain were all killed and I remained expiring on a heap of corpses. As every one knows, such scenes go on in an area of more than three hundred square leagues [6]

6. **league** Three geographical miles.

and yet no one ever fails to recite the five daily prayers ordered by Mahomet.

"With great difficulty I extricated myself from the bloody
heaps of corpses and dragged myself to the foot of a large
orange tree on the bank of a stream; there I fell down with   100
terror, weariness, horror, despair and hunger. Soon afterwards, my exhausted senses fell into a sleep which was
more like a swoon than repose. I was in this state of weakness and insensibility between life and death when I felt
myself oppressed by something which moved on my body.
I opened my eyes and saw a white man of good appearance
who was sighing and muttering between his teeth: *O che
sciagura d'essere senza coglioni!*

Chapter XII

CONTINUATION OF THE OLD
WOMAN'S MISFORTUNES

"Amazed and delighted to hear my native language, and not less surprised at the words spoken by this man, I re-plied that there were greater misfortunes than that of which he complained. In a few words I informed him of the horrors I had undergone and then swooned again. He carried me to a neighboring house, had me put to bed, gave me food, waited on me, consoled me, flattered me, told me he had never seen anyone so beautiful as I, and that he had never so much regretted that which no one could give back to him.

"'I was born at Naples,' he said, 'and every year they make two or three thousand children there into capons; some die of it, others acquire voices more beautiful than women's, and others become the governors of States. This operation was performed upon me with very great success and I was a musician in the chapel of the Princess of Palestrina.'

"'Of my mother,' I exclaimed.

"'Of your mother!' cried he, weeping. 'What! Are you that young princess I brought up to the age of six and who even then gave promise of being as beautiful as you are?'

"'I am! my mother is four hundred yards from here, cut into quarters under a heap of corpses . . .'

"I related all that had happened to me; he also told me his adventures and informed me how he had been sent to the King of Morocco by a Christian power to make a treaty with that monarch whereby he was supplied with powder, cannons and ships to help to exterminate the commerce of

other Christians. 'My mission is accomplished,' said this honest eunuch, 'I am about to embark at Ceuta and I will take   30
you back to Italy. *Ma che sciagura d'essere senza coglioni!'*

"I thanked him with tears of gratitude; and instead of
taking me back to Italy he conducted me to Algiers and sold
me to the Dey. I had scarcely been sold when the plague
which had gone through Africa, Asia and Europe, broke
out furiously in Algiers. You have seen earthquakes; but
have you ever seen the plague?"

"Never," replied the Baroness.

"If you had," replied the old woman, "you would admit
that it is much worse than an earthquake.[1] It is very com-   40
mon in Africa; I caught it. Imagine the situation of a Pope's
daughter aged fifteen, who in three months had undergone
poverty and slavery, had been raped nearly every day, had
seen her mother cut into four pieces, had undergone hunger
and war, and was now dying of the plague in Algiers. However, I did not die; but my eunuch and the Dey and almost
all the seraglio of Algiers perished.

"When the first ravages of this frightful plague were
over, the Dey's slaves were sold. A merchant bought me and
carried me to Tunis; he sold me to another merchant who   50
re-sold me at Tripoli; from Tripoli I was re-sold to Alexandria, from Alexandria re-sold to Smyrna, from Smyrna
to Constantinople. I was finally bought by an Aga of the
Janizaries,[2] who was soon ordered to defend Azov against
the Russians who were besieging it.

"The Aga, who was a man of great gallantry, took his
whole seraglio with him, and lodged us in a little fort on
the Islands of Palus-Maeotis,[3] guarded by two black eunuchs
and twenty soldiers. He killed a prodigious number of Russians but they returned the compliment as well. Azov was   60
given up to fire and blood, neither sex nor age was pardoned; only our little fort remained; and the enemy tried to
reduce it by starving us. The twenty Janizaries had sworn
never to surrender us. The extremities of hunger to which

1. **earthquake** As late as 1720, over 200,000 died of the plague in
Marseille.
2. **Janizaries** Footguards of the Turkish sultans.
3. **Maeotis** The Sea of Azov north of the Black Sea.

they were reduced forced them to eat our two eunuchs for
fear of breaking their oath. Some days later they resolved
to eat the women. We had with us a most pious and com-
passionate Imam who delivered a fine sermon to them by
which he persuaded them not to kill us altogether. 'Cut,'
70 said he, 'only one buttock from each of these ladies and you
will make very good cheer; if you have to return, there will
still be as much left in a few days; Heaven will be pleased
at so charitable an action and you will be saved.'

"He was very eloquent and persuaded them. This horrible operation was performed upon us; the Imam anointed
us with the same balm that is used for children who have
just been circumcised; we were all at the point of death.

"Scarcely had the Janizaries finished the meal we had
supplied when the Russians arrived in flat-bottomed boats;
80 not a Janizary escaped. The Russians paid no attention to
the state we were in. There are French doctors everywhere;
one of them who was very skilful, took care of us; he healed
us and I shall remember all my life that, when my wounds
were cured, he made propositions to me. For the rest, he
told us all to cheer up; he told us that the same thing had
happened in several sieges and that it was a law of war.

"As soon as my companions could walk they were sent
to Moscow. I fell to the lot of a Boyar who made me his
gardener and gave me twenty lashes a day. But at the end
90 of two years this lord was broken on the wheel with thirty
other Boyars owing to some court disturbance, and I
profited by this adventure; I fled; I crossed all Russia; for a
long time I was servant in an inn at Riga, then at Rostock,
at Wismar, at Leipzig, at Cassel, at Utrecht, at Leyden, at
the Hague, at Rotterdam; I have grown old in misery and
in shame, with only half a backside, always remembering
that I was the daughter of a Pope; a hundred times I
wanted to kill myself but I still loved life. This ridiculous
weakness is perhaps the most disastrous of our inclinations;
100 for is there anything sillier than to desire to bear continually
a burden one always wishes to throw on the ground; to
look upon oneself with horror and yet to cling to oneself;

in short, to caress the serpent which devours us until he has eaten our heart?

"In the countries it has been my fate to traverse and in the inns where I have served I have seen a prodigious number of people who hated their lives; but I have only seen twelve who voluntarily put an end to their misery: three negroes, four Englishmen, four Genevans and a German professor named Robeck.[4] I ended up as servant to the Jew, Don Issachar; he placed me in your service, my fair young lady; I attached myself to your fate and have been more occupied with your adventures than with my own. I should never even have spoken of my misfortunes, if you had not piqued me a little and if it had not been the custom on board ship to tell stories to pass the time. In short, Mademoiselle, I have had experience, I know the world; provide yourself with an entertainment, make each passenger tell you his story; and if there is one who has not often cursed his life, who has not often said to himself that he was the most unfortunate of men, throw me headfirst into the sea."

4. **Robeck** Robeck wrote a book in defense of suicide and later drowned himself (at the age of sixty-seven).

Chapter XIII

HOW CANDIDE WAS OBLIGED TO SEPARATE FROM THE FAIR CUNEGONDE AND THE OLD WOMAN

The fair Cunegonde, having heard the old woman's story, treated her with all the politeness due to a person of her rank and merit. She accepted the proposition and persuaded all the passengers one after the other to tell her their adventures. She and Candide admitted that the old woman was right.

"It was most unfortunate," said Candide, "that the wise Pangloss was hanged contrary to custom at an *auto-da-fé;* he would have said admirable things about the physical and
10 moral evils which cover the earth and the sea, and I should feel myself strong enough to urge a few objections with all due respect."

While each of the passengers was telling his story the ship proceeded on its way. They arrived at Buenos Ayres. Cunegonde, Captain Candide and the old woman went to call on the governor, Don Fernando d'Ibaraa y Figueora y Mascarenes y Lampourdos y Souza. This gentleman had the pride befitting a man who owned so many names. He talked to men with a most noble disdain, turning his nose
20 up so far, raising his voice so pitilessly, assuming so imposing a tone, affecting so lofty a carriage, that all who addressed him were tempted to give him a thrashing. He had a furious passion for women. Cunegonde seemed to him the most beautiful woman he had ever seen. The first thing he did was to ask if she were the Captain's wife. The air with which he asked this question alarmed Candide; he

did not dare say that she was his wife, because as a matter of fact she was not; he dared not say she was his sister, because she was not that either; and though this official lie was formerly extremely fashionable among the ancients,[1] 30 and might be useful to the moderns, his soul was too pure to depart from truth.

"Mademoiselle Cunegonde," said he, "is about to do me the honor of marrying me, and we beg your excellency to be present at the wedding."

Don Fernando d'Ibaraa y Figueora y Mascarenes y Lampourdos y Souza twisted his moustache, smiled bitterly and ordered Captain Candide to go and inspect his company. Candide obeyed; the governor remained with Mademoiselle Cunegonde. He declared his passion, vowed that the next 40 day he would marry her publicly, or otherwise, as it might please her charms. Cunegonde asked for a quarter of an hour to collect herself, to consult the old woman and to make up her mind.

The old woman said to Cunegonde: "You have seventy-two quarterings and you haven't a shilling; it is in your power to be the wife of the greatest Lord in South America, who has an exceedingly fine moustache; is it for you to pride yourself on a rigid fidelity? You have been raped by Bulgarians, a Jew and an Inquisitor have enjoyed your good 50 graces; misfortunes confer certain rights. If I were in your place, I confess I should not have the least scruple in marrying the governor and making Captain Candide's fortune."

While the old woman was speaking with all that prudence which comes from age and experience, they saw a small ship come into the harbor; an Alcayde and some Alguazils were on board, and this is what had happened. The old woman had guessed correctly that it was a long-sleeved monk who stole Cunegonde's money and jewels at Badajoz, when she was flying in all haste with Candide. 60 The monk tried to sell some of the gems to a jeweller. The merchant recognised them as the property of the Grand

1. **ancients** I.e., among the Israelites. A veiled allusion to Abraham and Sarah.

Inquisitor. Before the monk was hanged he confessed that
he had stolen them; he described the persons and the direction they were taking. The flight of Cunegonde and
Candide was already known. They were followed to Cadiz;
without any waste of time a vessel was sent in pursuit of
them. The vessel was already in the harbor at Buenos Ayres.
The rumor spread that an Alcayde was about to land and
70 that he was in pursuit of the murderers of His Lordship the
Grand Inquisitor. The prudent old woman saw in a moment what was to be done.

"You cannot escape," she said to Cunegonde, "and you
have nothing to fear; you did not kill His Lordship; moreover, the governor is in love with you and will not allow
you to be maltreated; stay here."

She ran to Candide at once. "Fly," said she, "or in an
hour's time you will be burned." There was not a moment
to lose; but how could he leave Cunegonde and where could
80 he take refuge?

Chapter XIV

HOW CANDIDE AND CACAMBO WERE
RECEIVED BY THE JESUITS
IN PARAGUAY

Candide had brought from Cadiz a valet of a sort which is very common on the coasts of Spain and in the colonies He was one-quarter Spanish, the child of a half-breed in Tucuman;[1] he had been a choirboy, a sacristan, a sailor, a monk, a postman, a soldier and a lackey. His name was Cacambo and he loved his master because his master was a very good man. He saddled the two Andalusian horses with all speed. "Come, master, we must follow the old woman's advice; let us be off and ride without looking behind us."

Candide shed tears. "O my dear Cunegonde! Must I abandon you just when the governor was about to marry us! Cunegonde, brought here from such a distant land, what will become of you?"

"She will become what she can," said Cacambo. "Women never trouble about themselves; God will see to her. Let us be off."

"Where are you taking me? Where are we going? What shall we do without Cunegonde?" said Candide.

"By St. James of Compostella," said Cacambo, "you were going to fight the Jesuits; let us go and fight for them; I know the roads, I will take you to their kingdom, they will be charmed to have a captain who can drill in the Bulgarian fashion; you will make a prodigious fortune; when a man fails in one world, he succeeds in another. 'Tis a very great pleasure to see and do new things."

1. **Tucuman** Argentinian province.

"Then you have been in Paraguay?" said Candide.

"Yes, indeed," said Cacambo. "I was servitor in the College of the Assumption, and I know the government of *Los
Padres*[2] as well as I know the streets of Cadiz. Their government is a most admirable thing. The kingdom is already
more than three hundred leagues in diameter and is divided
into thirty provinces. *Los Padres* have everything and the
people have nothing; 'tis the masterpiece of reason and justice. For my part, I know nothing so divine as *Los Padres*
who here make war on the Kings of Spain and Portugal
and in Europe act as their confessors; who here kill Spaniards and at Madrid send them to Heaven; all this delights
me; come on; you will be the happiest of men. What a
pleasure it will be to *Los Padres* when they know there is
coming to them a captain who can drill in the Bulgarian
manner!"

As soon as they reached the first barrier, Cacambo told
the picket that a captain wished to speak to the Commandant. This information was carried to the main guard. A
Paraguayan officer ran to the feet of the Commandant to
tell him the news. Candide and Cacambo were disarmed
and their two Andalusian horses were taken from them.
The two strangers were brought in between two ranks of
soldiers; the Commandant was at the end, with a three-
cornered hat on his head, his gown tucked up, a sword at
his side and a spontoon[3] in his hand. He made a sign
and immediately the two newcomers were surrounded by
twenty-four soldiers. A sergeant told them that they must
wait, that the Commandant could not speak to them, that
the reverend provincial father did not allow any Spaniard
to open his mouth in his presence or to remain more than
three hours in the country.

"And where is the reverend provincial father?" said Cacambo.

"He is on parade after having said Mass, and you will

2. **Los padres** Spanish for the (Jesuit) Fathers.
3. **spontoon** A half-pike.

have to wait three hours before you will be allowed to kiss his spurs."

"But," said Cacambo, "the captain, who is dying of hunger just as I am, is not a Spaniard but a German; can we not break our fast while we are waiting for his reverence?"

The sergeant went at once to inform the Commandant of this.

"Blessed be God!" said that lord. "Since he is a German I can speak to him; bring him to my arbor."   70

Candide was immediately taken to a leafy summerhouse decorated with a very pretty colonnade of green marble and gold, and lattices enclosing parrots, hummingbirds, colibris,[4] guinea hens and many other rare birds. An excellent breakfast stood ready in gold dishes; and while the Paraguayans were eating maize from wooden bowls, out of doors and in the heat of the sun, the reverend father Commandant entered the arbor.

He was a very handsome young man, with a full face, a fairly white skin, red cheeks, arched eyebrows, keen eyes,   80 red ears, vermilion lips, a haughty air, but a haughtiness which was neither that of a Spaniard nor of a Jesuit. Candide and Cacambo were given back the arms which had been taken from them and their two Andalusian horses; Cacambo fed them with oats near the arbor, and kept his eye on them for fear of a surprise. Candide first kissed the hem of the Commandant's gown and then they sat down to table. "So you are a German?" said the Jesuit in that language.

"Yes, reverend father," said Candide.   90

As they spoke these words they gazed at each other with extreme surprise and an emotion they could not control.

"And what part of Germany do you come from?" said the Jesuit.

"From the filthy province of Westphalia," said Candide; "I was born in the castle of Thunder-ten-tronckh."

"Heavens! Is it possible!" cried the Commandant.

4. colibris A species of hummingbird.

"What a miracle!" cried Candide.

"Can it be you?" said the Commandant.

100 " 'Tis impossible!" said Candide. They both fell over backwards, embraced and shed rivers of tears.[5]

"What! Can it be you, reverend father? You, the fair Cunegonde's brother! You, who were killed by the Bulgarians! You, the son of My Lord the Baron! You, a Jesuit in Paraguay! The world is indeed a strange place! O Pangloss! Pangloss! How happy you would have been if you had not been hanged!"

The Commandant sent away the negro slaves and the Paraguayans who were serving wine in goblets of rock
110 crystal. A thousand times did he thank God and St. Ignatius; [6] he clasped Candide in his arms; their faces were wet with tears.

"You would be still more surprised, more touched, more beside yourself," said Candide, "if I were to tell you that Mademoiselle Cunegonde, your sister, whom you thought disembowelled, is in the best of health."

"Where?"

"In your neighborhood, with the governor of Buenos Ayres; and I came to make war on you."

120 Every word they spoke in this long conversation piled marvel on marvel. Their whole souls flew from their tongues, listened in their ears and sparkled in their eyes. As they were Germans, they sat at table for a long time, waiting for the reverend father provincial; and the Commandant spoke as follows to his dear Candide.

5. **tears** A parody again of recognition scenes.
6. **Ignatius** Ignatius de Loyola, founder of the Jesuit order.

Chapter XV

HOW CANDIDE KILLED HIS DEAR
CUNEGONDE'S BROTHER

"I shall remember all my life the horrible day when I saw my father and mother killed and my sister raped. When the Bulgarians had gone, my adorable sister could not be found, and my mother, my father and I, two maidservants and three little murdered boys were placed in a cart to be buried in a Jesuit chapel two leagues from the castle of my fathers. A Jesuit sprinkled us with holy water; it was horribly salt; a few drops fell in my eyes; the father noticed that my eyelids trembled, he put his hand on my heart and felt that it was still beating; I was attended to and at the end of three weeks was as well as if nothing had happened. You know, my dear Candide, that I was a very pretty youth, and I became still prettier; and so the Reverend Father Croust, the Superior of the house, was inspired with a most tender friendship for me; he gave me the dress of a novice and some time afterwards I was sent to Rome. The Father General wished to recruit some young German Jesuits. The sovereigns of Paraguay take as few Spanish Jesuits as they can; they prefer foreigners, whom they think they can control better. The Reverend Father General thought me apt to labor in his vineyard. I set off with a Pole and a Tyrolese. When I arrived I was honored with a subdeaconship and a lieutenancy; I am now colonel and priest. We shall give the King of Spain's troops a warm reception; I guarantee they will be excommunicated and beaten. Providence has sent you to help us. But is it really true that my dear sister Cunegonde is in the neighborhood with the governor of Buenos Ayres?"

45

Candide assured him on oath that nothing could be truer.
30 Their tears began to flow once more. The Baron seemed
never to grow tired of embracing Candide; he called him
his brother, his savior.

"Ah! My dear Candide," said he, "perhaps we shall enter
the town together as conquerors and regain my sister Cunegonde."

"I desire it above all things," said Candide, "for I meant
to marry her and I still hope to do so."

"You, insolent wretch!" replied the Baron. "Would you
have the impudence to marry my sister who has seventy-two
40 quarterings! I consider you extremely impudent to dare to
speak to me of such a foolhardy intention!"

Candide, petrified at this speech, replied: "Reverend
Father, all the quarterings in the world are of no impor-
tance; I rescued your sister from the arms of a Jew and an
Inquisitor; she is under considerable obligation to me and
wishes to marry me. Dr. Pangloss always said that men are
equal and I shall certainly marry her."

"We shall see about that, scoundrel!" said the Jesuit
Baron of Thunder-ten-tronckh, at the same time hitting
50 him violently in the face with the flat of his sword. Candide
promptly drew his own and stuck it up to the hilt in the
Jesuit Baron's belly; but, as he drew it forth smoking, he
began to weep. "Alas! My God," said he, "I have killed
my old master, my friend, my brother-in-law; I am the
mildest man in the world and I have already killed three
men, two of them priests."

Cacambo, who was acting as sentry at the door of the
arbor, ran in.

"There is nothing left for us but to sell our lives dearly,"
60 said his master. "Somebody will certainly come into the
arbor and we must die weapon in hand."

Cacambo, who had seen this sort of thing before, did not
lose his head; he took off the Baron's Jesuit gown, put it on
Candide, gave him the dead man's square bonnet, and made
him mount a horse. All this was done in the twinkling of
an eye. "Let us gallop, master; every one will take you for

a Jesuit carrying orders and we shall have passed the frontiers before they can pursue us."

As he spoke these words he started off at full speed and shouted in Spanish: "Way, way for the Reverend Father Colonel . . ." 70

Chapter XVI

WHAT HAPPENED TO THE TWO TRAVELLERS WITH TWO GIRLS, TWO MONKEYS, AND THE SAVAGES CALLED OREILLONS

Candide and his valet were past the barriers before anybody in the camp knew of the death of the German Jesuit. The vigilant Cacambo had taken care to fill his saddlebag with bread, chocolate, ham, fruit, and several bottles of wine. On their Andalusian horses they plunged into an unknown country where they found no road. At last a beautiful plain traversed by streams met their eyes. Our two travellers put their horses to grass. Cacambo suggested to his master that they should eat and set the example.

10   "How can you expect me to eat ham," said Candide, "when I have killed the son of My Lord the Baron and find myself condemned never to see the fair Cunegonde again in my life? What is the use of prolonging my miserable days since I must drag them out far from her in remorse and despair? And what will the Journal de Trévoux [1] say?"

Speaking thus, he began to eat. The sun was setting. The two wanderers heard faint cries which seemed to be uttered by women. They could not tell whether these were cries of pain or of joy; but they rose hastily with that alarm and uneasiness caused by everything in an unknown country.
20   These cries came from two completely naked girls who were running gently along the edge of the plain, while two monkeys pursued them and bit their buttocks. Candide was

1. **Trévoux** The celebrated Journal of the French Jesuits. Voltaire often satirized its editor.

moved to pity; he had learned to shoot among the Bulgarians and could have brought down a nut from a tree without touching the leaves. He raised his double-barrelled Spanish gun, fired, and killed the two monkeys.

"God be praised, my dear Cacambo, I have delivered these two poor creatures from a great danger; if I committed a sin by killing an Inquisitor and a Jesuit, I have atoned for it by saving the lives of these two girls. Perhaps they are young ladies of quality and this adventure may be of great advantage to us in this country."

He was going on, but his tongue clove to the roof of his mouth when he saw the two girls tenderly kissing the two monkeys, shedding tears on their bodies and filling the air with the most piteous cries.

"I did not expect so much human kindliness," he said at last to Cacambo, who replied: "You have performed a wonderful masterpiece; you have killed the two lovers of these young ladies."

"Their lovers! Can it be possible? You are jesting at me, Cacambo; how can I believe you?"

"My dear master," replied Cacambo, "you are always surprised by everything; why should you think it so strange that in some countries there should be monkeys who obtain ladies' favors? They are quarter men, as I am a quarter Spaniard."

"Alas!" replied Candide, "I remember to have heard Dr. Pangloss say that similar accidents occurred in the past and that these mixtures produce Aigypans, fauns and satyrs; that several eminent persons of antiquity have seen them; but I thought they were fables." [2]

"You ought now to be convinced that it is true," said Cacambo, "and you see how people behave when they have not received a proper education; the only thing I fear is that these ladies may get us into difficulty."

These wise reflections persuaded Candide to leave the plain and to plunge into the woods. He ate supper there with

2. fables Voltaire had read these stories in a serious book on mythology by Abbé Banier.

60 Cacambo and, after having cursed the Inquisitor of Portugal, the governor of Buenos Ayres and the Baron, they went
to sleep on the moss. When they woke up they found they
could not move; the reason was that during the night the
Oreillons,[3] the inhabitants of the country, to whom they
had been denounced by the two ladies, had bound them
with ropes made of bark. They were surrounded by fifty
naked Oreillons, armed with arrows, clubs and stone
hatchets. Some were boiling a large cauldron, others were
preparing spits and they were all shouting: "Here's a Jesuit,
70 here's a Jesuit! We shall be revenged and have a good dinner; let us eat the Jesuit, let us eat the Jesuit!" [4]

"I told you so, my dear master," said Cacambo sadly. "I
knew those two girls would play us a dirty trick."

Candide perceived the cauldron and the spits and exclaimed: "We are certainly going to be roasted or boiled.
Ah! What would Dr. Pangloss say if he saw what the pure
state of nature is? All is well, granted; but I confess it is
very cruel to have lost Mademoiselle Cunegonde and to be
spitted by the Oreillons."

80 Cacambo never lost his head. "Do not despair," he said
to the wretched Candide. "I understand a little of their dia-
lect and I will speak to them."

"Do not fail," said Candide, "to point out to them the
dreadful inhumanity of cooking men and how very un-
christian it is."

"Gentlemen," said Cacambo, "you mean to eat a Jesuit
today? 'Tis a good deed; nothing could be more just than
to treat one's enemies in this fashion.[5] Indeed the law of
nature teaches us to kill our neighbor and this is how peo-
90 ple behave all over the world. If we do not exert the right
of eating our neighbor, it is because we have other means

3. **Oreillons** A tribe of Indians, so called because they distended
their ears with ornaments.

4. **Jesuit** The translation should read: "Let us eat Jesuit." The Jesuits were expelled from France five years after *Candide*—but not because of *Candide*.

5. **fashion** It was in fact a common practice among American Indians, a way of acquiring an enemy's valor.

of making good cheer; but you have not the same resources as we, and it is certainly better to eat our enemies than to abandon the fruits of victory to ravens and crows. But, gentlemen, you would not wish to eat your friends. You believe you are about to place a Jesuit on the spit, and 'tis your defender, the enemy of your enemies you are about to roast. I was born in your country; the gentleman you see here is my master and, far from being a Jesuit, he has just killed a Jesuit and is wearing his clothes; which is the cause 100 of your mistake. To verify what I say, take his gown, carry it to the first barrier of the kingdom of *Los Padres* and inquire whether my master has not killed a Jesuit officer. It will not take you long and you will have plenty of time to eat us if you find I have lied. But if I have told the truth, you are too well acquainted with the principles of public law, good morals and discipline, not to pardon us."

The Oreillons thought this a very reasonable speech; they deputed two of their notables to go with all diligence and find out the truth. The two deputies acquitted themselves 110 of their task like intelligent men and soon returned with the good news. The Oreillons unbound their two prisoners, overwhelmed them with civilities, offered them girls, gave them refreshment, and accompanied them to the frontiers of their dominions, shouting joyfully: "He is not a Jesuit, he is not a Jesuit!"

Candide could not cease from wondering at the cause of his deliverance. "What a nation," said he. "What men! What manners! If I had not been so lucky as to stick my sword through the body of Mademoiselle Cunegonde's 120 brother I should infallibly have been eaten. But, after all, there is something good in the pure state of nature, since these people, instead of eating me, offered me a thousand civilities as soon as they knew I was not a Jesuit."

Chapter XVII

ARRIVAL OF CANDIDE AND HIS VALET IN THE COUNTRY OF ELDORADO [1] AND WHAT THEY SAW THERE

When they reached the frontiers of the Oreillons, Cacambo said to Candide: "You see this hemisphere is no better than the other; take my advice, let us go back to Europe by the shortest road."

"How can we go back," said Candide, "and where can we go? If I go to my own country, the Bulgarians and the Abares are murdering everybody; if I return to Portugal I shall be burned; if we stay here, we run the risk of being spitted at any moment. But how can I make up my mind
10 to leave that part of the world where Mademoiselle Cunegonde is living?"

"Let us go to Cayenne," [2] said Cacambo, "we shall find Frenchmen there, for they go all over the world; they might help us. Perhaps God will have pity on us."

It was not easy to go to Cayenne. They knew roughly the direction to take, but mountains, rivers, precipices, brigands and savages were everywhere terrible obstacles. Their horses died of fatigue; their provisions were exhausted; for a whole month they lived on wild fruits and at last found them-
20 selves near a little river fringed with cocoanut-trees which supported their lives and their hopes.

Cacambo, who always gave advice as prudent as the old woman's, said to Candide: "We can go no farther, we have walked far enough; I can see an empty canoe in the bank,

1. **Eldorado** A fabulous Land of Gold, in which even Sir Walter Raleigh once believed.
2. **Cayenne** Capital of French Guiana.

let us fill it with cocoanuts, get into the little boat and drift
with the current; a river always leads to some inhabited
place. If we do not find anything pleasant, we shall at least
find something new."

"Come on then," said Candide, "and let us trust to Provi-
dence."   30

They drifted for some leagues between banks which were
sometimes flowery, sometimes bare, sometimes flat, sometimes steep. The river continually became wider; finally it
disappeared under an arch of frightful rocks which towered
up to the very sky. The two travellers were bold enough to
trust themselves to the current under this arch. The stream,
narrowed between walls, carried them with horrible rapidity
and noise. After twenty-four hours they saw daylight again;
but their canoe was wrecked on reefs; they had to crawl
from rock to rock for a whole league and at last they   40
discovered an immense horizon, bordered by inaccessible
mountains. The country was cultivated for pleasure as well
as for necessity; everywhere the useful was agreeable. The
roads were covered or rather ornamented with carriages of
brilliant material and shape, carrying men and women of
singular beauty, who were rapidly drawn along by large
red sheep whose swiftness surpassed that of the finest horses
of Andalusia, Tetuan, and Mequinez.[3]

"This country," said Candide, "is better than West-
phalia."   50

He landed with Cacambo near the first village he came
to. Several children of the village, dressed in torn gold bro-
cade, were playing quoits outside the village. Our two men
from the other world amused themselves by looking on;
their quoits were large round pieces, yellow, red and green
which shone with peculiar lustre. The travellers were curious enough to pick up some of them; they were of gold,
emeralds and rubies, the least of which would have been
the greatest ornament in the Mogul's throne.

3. **Mequinez** Tetuan and Mequinez are Moroccan towns.

60   "No doubt," said Cacambo, "these children are the sons
of the King of this country playing at quoits."

At that moment the village schoolmaster appeared to call
them into school.

"This," said Candide, "is the tutor of the Royal Family."

The little beggars immediately left their game, abandon-
ing their quoits and everything with which they had been
playing. Candide picked them up, ran to the tutor, and presented them to him humbly, giving him to understand by
signs that their Royal Highnesses had forgotten their gold
70   and their precious stones. The village schoolmaster smiled,
threw them on the ground, gazed for a moment at Candide's face with much surprise and continued on his way.
The travellers did not fail to pick up the gold, the rubies
and the emeralds.

"Where are we?" cried Candide. "The children of the
King must be well brought up, since they are taught to
despise gold and precious stones."

Cacambo was as much surprised as Candide. At last they
reached the first house in the village, which was built like
80   a European palace. There were crowds of people round the
door and still more inside; very pleasant music could be
heard and there was a delicious smell of cooking. Cacambo
went up to the door and heard them speaking Peruvian; it
was his maternal tongue, for everyone knows that Cacambo
was born in a village of Tucuman where nothing else *is*
spoken.

"I will act as your interpreter," he said to Candide, "this
is an inn, let us enter."

Immediately two boys and two girls of the inn, dressed
90   in cloth of gold, whose hair was bound up with ribbons,
invited them to sit down to the table d'hôte. They served
four soups each garnished with two parrots, a boiled condor
which weighed two hundred pounds, two roast monkeys of
excellent flavor, three hundred colibris in one dish and six
hundred hummingbirds in another, exquisite ragouts and
delicious pastries, all in dishes of a sort of rock crystal. The
boys and girls brought several sorts of drinks made of sugar-

cane. Most of the guests were merchants and coachmen, all extremely polite, who asked Cacambo a few questions with the most delicate discretion and answered his in a satisfac- 100 tory manner.

When the meal was over, Cacambo, like Candide, thought he could pay the reckoning by throwing on the table two of the large pieces of gold he had picked up; the host and hostess laughed until they had to hold their sides. At last they recovered themselves.

"Gentlemen," said the host, "we perceive you are strangers; we are not accustomed to seeing them. Forgive us if we began to laugh when you offered us in payment the stones from our highways. No doubt you have none of the 110 money of this country, but you do not need any to dine here. All the hotels established for the utility of commerce are paid for by the government. You have been ill entertained here because this is a poor village; but everywhere else you will be received as you deserve to be."

Cacambo explained to Candide all that the host had said, and Candide listened in the same admiration and disorder with which his friend Cacambo interpreted. "What can this country be," they said to each other, "which is unknown to the rest of the world and where all nature is so different 120 from ours? Probably it is the country where everything is for the best; for there must be one country of that sort. And, in spite of what Dr. Pangloss said, I often noticed that everything went very ill in Westphalia."

Chapter XVIII

WHAT THEY SAW IN THE LAND
OF ELDORADO

Cacambo informed the host of his curiosity, and the host said: "I am a very ignorant man and am all the better for it; but we have here an old man who has retired from the court and who is the most learned and most communicative man in the kingdom." And he at once took Cacambo to the old man. Candide now played only the second part and accompanied his valet. They entered a very simple house, for the door was only of silver and the panelling of the apartments in gold, but so tastefully carved that the richest decorations did not surpass it. The antechamber indeed was only encrusted with rubies and emeralds; but the order with which everything was arranged atoned for this extreme simplicity.

The old man received the two strangers on a sofa padded with colibri feathers, and presented them with drinks in diamond cups; after which he satisfied their curiosity in these words: "I am a hundred and seventy-two years old and I heard from my late father, the King's equerry, the astonishing revolutions of Peru of which he had been an eye-witness. The kingdom where we now are is the ancient country of the Incas, who most imprudently left it to conquer part of the world and were at last destroyed by the Spaniards. The princes of their family who remained in their native country had more wisdom; with the consent of the nation, they ordered that no inhabitants should ever leave our little kingdom, and this it is that has preserved our innocence and our felicity. The Spaniards had some vague knowledge of this country, which they called Eldo rado, and about a hundred years ago an Englishman named Raleigh came very near to it; but, since we are surrounded by inaccessible rocks and precipices, we have hitherto been exempt from the rapacity of the nations of Europe who have an inconceivable lust for the pebbles and mud of our land and would kill us to the last man to get possession of them."

The conversation was long; it touched upon the form of the government, manners, women, public spectacles and the arts. Finally Candide, who was always interested in metaphysics, asked through Cacambo whether the country had a religion.

The old man blushed a little. "How can you doubt it?" said he. "Do you think we are ingrates?"

Cacambo humbly asked what was the religion of Eldorado.

The old man blushed again. "Can there be two religions?" said he. "We have, I think, the religion of every one else; we adore God from evening until morning."

"Do you adore only one God?" said Cacambo, who continued to act as the interpreter of Candide's doubts.

"Manifestly," said the old man, "there are not two or three or four. I must confess that the people of your world ask very extraordinary questions."

Candide continued to press the old man with questions; he wished to know how they prayed to God in Eldorado.

"We do not pray," said the good and respectable sage, "we have nothing to ask from him; he has given us everything necessary and we continually give him thanks."

Candide was curious to see the priests; and asked where they were.

The good old man smiled. "My friends," said he, "we are all priests; the King and all the heads of families solemnly sing praises every morning, accompanied by five or six thousand musicians."

"What! Have you no monks to teach, to dispute, to govern, to intrigue and to burn people who do not agree with them?"

"For that, we should have to become fools," said the old man; "here we are all of the same opinion and do not understand what you mean with your monks."

70   At all this Candide was in an ecstasy and said to himself: "This is very different from Westphalia and the castle of His Lordship the Baron; if our friend Pangloss had seen Eldorado, he would not have said that the castle of Thunder-ten-tronckh was the best of all that exists on the earth; certainly, a man should travel."

After this long conversation the good old man ordered a carriage to be harnessed with six sheep and gave the two travellers twelve of his servants to take them to court. "You will excuse me," he said, "if my age deprives me of the

80   honor of accompanying you. The King will receive you in a manner which will not displease you and doubtless you will pardon the customs of the country if any of them disconcert you."

Candide and Cacambo entered the carriage; the six sheep galloped off and in less than four hours they reached the King's palace, which was situated at one end of the capital. The portal was two hundred and twenty feet high and a hundred feet wide; it is impossible to describe its material. Anyone can see the prodigious superiority it must have over

90   the pebbles and sand we call *gold* and *gems*.

Twenty beautiful maidens of the guard received Candide and Cacambo as they alighted from the carriage, conducted them to the baths and dressed them in robes woven from the down of colibris; after which the principal male and female officers of the Crown led them to his Majesty's apartment through two files of a thousand musicians each, according to the usual custom. As they approached the throneroom, Cacambo asked one of the chief officers how they should behave in his Majesty's presence; whether they

100   should fall on their knees or flat on their faces, whether they should put their hands on their heads or on their backsides; whether they should lick the dust of the throneroom; in a word, what was the ceremony?

"The custom," said the chief officer, "is to embrace the King and to kiss him on either cheek."

Candide and Cacambo threw their arms round his Majesty's neck; he received them with all imaginable favor and politely asked them to supper. Meanwhile they were carried to see the town, the public buildings rising to the very skies, the market-places ornamented with thousands of columns, 110 the fountains of rose-water and of liquors distilled from sugarcane, which played continually in the public squares paved with precious stones which emitted a perfume like that of cloves and cinnamon.

Candide asked to see the law courts; he was told there were none, and that nobody ever went to law. He asked if there were prisons and was told there were none. He was still more surprised and pleased by the palace of sciences, where he saw a gallery two thousand feet long, filled with instruments of mathematics and physics.   120

After they had explored all the afternoon about a thousandth part of the town, they were taken back to the King. Candide sat down to table with his Majesty, his valet Cacambo and several ladies. Never was better cheer, and never was anyone wittier at supper than his Majesty. Cacambo explained the King's witty remarks to Candide and even when translated they still appeared witty. Among all the things which amazed Candide, this did not amaze him the least.

They enjoyed this hospitality for a month. Candide re- 13ᶜ peatedly said to Cacambo: "Once again, my friend, it is quite true that the castle where I was born cannot be compared with this country; but then Mademoiselle Cunegonde is not here and you probably have a mistress in Europe. If we remain here, we shall only be like everyone else; but if we return to our own world with only twelve sheep laden with Eldorado pebbles, we shall be richer than all the kings put together; we shall have no more Inquisitors to fear and we can easily regain Mademoiselle Cunegonde."

Cacambo agreed with this; it is so pleasant to be on the 14ᶜ move, to show off before friends, to make a parade of the

things seen on one's travels, that these two happy men resolved to be so no longer and to ask his Majesty's permission to depart.

"You are doing a very silly thing," said the King. "I
know my country is small; but when we are comfortable
anywhere we should stay there; I certainly have not the
right to detain foreigners, that is a tyranny which does not
exist either in our manners or our laws; all men are free,
150 leave when you please, but the way out is very difficult. It
is impossible to ascend the rapid river by which you mirac-
ulously came here and which flows under arches of rock.
The mountains which surround the whole of my kingdom
are ten thousand feet high and are perpendicular like walls;
they are more than ten leagues broad, and you can only get
down from them by way of precipices. However, since you
must go, I will give orders to the directors of machinery to
make a machine which will carry you comfortably. When
you have been taken to the other side of the mountains, no-
160 body can proceed any farther with you; for my subjects
have sworn never to pass this boundary and they are too
wise to break their oath. Ask anything else of me you wish."

"We ask nothing of your Majesty," said Cacambo, "except a few sheep laden with provisions, pebbles and the
mud of this country."

The King laughed. "I cannot understand," said he, "the
taste you people of Europe have for our yellow mud; but
take as much as you wish, and much good may it do you."

He immediately ordered his engineers to make a machine
170 to hoist these two extraordinary men out of his kingdom.
Three thousand learned scientists worked at it; it was ready
in a fortnight and only cost about twenty million pounds
sterling in the money of that country. Candide and Cacambo
were placed on the machine; there were two large red sheep
saddled and bridled for them to ride on when they had
passed the mountains, twenty sumpter sheep [1] laden with
provisions, thirty carrying presents of the most curious pro-

1. sheep Pack-sheep.

ductions of the country and fifty laden with gold, precious stones and diamonds. The King embraced the two vagabonds tenderly. Their departure was a splendid sight and so was the ingenious manner in which they and their sheep were hoisted on to the top of the mountains. The scientists took leave of them after having landed them safely, and Candide's only desire and object was to go and present Mademoiselle Cunegonde with his sheep.

"We have sufficient to pay the governor of Buenos Ayres," said he, "if Mademoiselle Cunegonde can be bought. Let us go to Cayenne, and take ship, and then we will see what kingdom we will buy."

Chapter XIX

WHAT HAPPENED TO THEM AT SURINAM AND HOW CANDIDE MADE THE ACQUAINTANCE OF MARTIN

Our two travellers' first day was quite pleasant. They were encouraged by the idea of possessing more treasures than all Asia, Europe and Africa could collect. Candide in transport carved the name of Cunegonde on the trees. On the second day two of the sheep stuck in a marsh and were swallowed up with their loads; two other sheep died of fatigue a few days later; then seven or eight died of hunger in a desert; several days afterwards others fell off precipices. Finally, after they had travelled for a hundred days, they had only two sheep left.

Candide said to Cacambo: "My friend, you see how perishable are the riches of this world; nothing is steadfast but virtue and the happiness of seeing Mademoiselle Cunegonde again."

"I admit it," said Cacambo, "but we still have two sheep with more treasures than ever the King of Spain will have, and in the distance I see a town I suspect is Surinam,¹ which belongs to the Dutch. We are at the end of our troubles and the beginning of our happiness."

As they drew near the town they came upon a negro lying on the ground wearing only half his clothes, that is to say, a pair of blue cotton drawers; this poor man had no left leg and no right hand. "Good heavens!" said Candide to him in Dutch, "what are you doing there, my friend, in that horrible state?"

10

20

1. **Surinam** In Dutch Guiana.

"I am waiting for my master, the famous merchant Monsieur Vanderdendur."

"Was it Monsieur Vanderdendur," said Candide, "who treated you in that way?"

"Yes, sir," said the negro, "it is the custom. We are given a pair of cotton drawers twice a year as clothing. When we work in the sugar mills and the grindstone catches our fingers, they cut off the hand; when we try to run away, they cut off a leg. Both these things happened to me. This is the price paid for the sugar you eat in Europe. But when my mother sold me for ten patagons on the coast of Guinea, she said to me: 'My dear child, give thanks to our fetishes, always worship them, and they will make you happy; you have the honor to be a slave of our lords the white men and thereby you have made the fortune of your father and mother.' Alas! I do not know whether I made their fortune, but they certainly did not make mine. Dogs, monkeys and parrots are a thousand times less miserable than we are; the Dutch fetishes who converted me tell me that we are all of us, whites and blacks, the children of Adam. I am not a genealogist, but if these preachers tell the truth, we are all second cousins. Now, you will admit that no one could treat his relatives in a more horrible way."

"O Pangloss!" cried Candide. "This is an abomination you had not guessed; this is too much, in the end I shall have to renounce optimism."

"What is optimism?" said Cacambo.

"Alas!" said Candide, "it is the mania of maintaining that everything is well when we are wretched." [2] And he shed tears as he looked at his negro; and he entered Surinam weeping.

The first thing they inquired was whether there was any ship in the port which could be sent to Buenos Ayres. The person they addressed happened to be a Spanish captain, who offered to strike an honest bargain with them. He arranged to meet them at an inn. Candide and the faith-

2. **wretched** This is Voltaire's main point. Happiness in the abstract has no meaning for the suffering individual.

ful Cacambo went and waited for him with their two sheep. Candide, who blurted everything out, told the Spaniard all his adventures and confessed that he wanted to elope with Mademoiselle Cunegonde.

"I shall certainly not take you to Buenos Ayres," said the captain. "I should be hanged and you would, too. The fair Cunegonde is his Lordship's favorite mistress."

Candide was thunderstruck; he sobbed for a long time; 70 then he took Cacambo aside. "My dear friend," said he, "this is what you must do. We have each of us in our pockets five or six millions worth of diamonds; you are more skilful than I am; go to Buenos Ayres and get Mademoiselle Cunegonde. If the governor makes any difficulties give him a million; if he is still obstinate give him two; you have not killed an Inquisitor so they will not suspect you. I will fit out another ship, I will go and wait for you at Venice; it is a free country where there is nothing to fear from Bulgarians, Abares, Jews or Inquisitors."

80 Cacambo applauded this wise resolution; he was in despair at leaving a good master who had become his intimate friend; but the pleasure of being useful to him overcame the grief of leaving him. They embraced with tears. Candide urged him not to forget the good old woman. Cacambo set off that very same day; he was a very good man, this Cacambo.

Candide remained some time longer at Surinam waiting for another captain to take him to Italy with the two sheep he had left. He engaged servants and bought everything 90 necessary for a long voyage. At last Monsieur Vanderdendur, the owner of a large ship, came to see him.

"How much do you want," he asked this man, "to take me straight to Venice with my servants, my baggage and these two sheep?"

The captain asked for ten thousand piastres. Candide did not hesitate. "Oh! Ho!" said the prudent Vanderdendur to himself, "this foreigner gives ten thousand piastres immediately! He must be very rich." He returned a moment aft-

erwards and said he could not sail for less than twenty
thousand. 100

"Very well, you shall have them," said Candide.

"Whew!" said the merchant to himself, "this man gives
twenty thousand piastres as easily as ten thousand." He
came back again, and said he could not take him to Venice
for less than thirty thousand piastres.

"Then you shall have thirty thousand," replied Candide.

"Oho!" said the Dutch merchant to himself again, "thirty
thousand piastres is nothing to this man; obviously the two
sheep are laden with immense treasures; I will not insist
any further; first let me make him pay the thirty thousand 110
piastres, and then we will see."

Candide sold two little diamonds, the smaller of which
was worth more than all the money the captain asked. He
paid him in advance. The two sheep were taken on board.
Candide followed in a little boat to join the ship which rode
at anchor; the captain watched his time, set his sails and
weighed anchor; the wind was favorable. Candide, bewildered and stupefied, soon lost sight of him. "Alas!" he cried,
"this is a trick worthy of the old world."

He returned to shore, in grief; for he had lost enough to 120
make the fortunes of twenty kings. He went to the Dutch
judge; and, as he was rather disturbed, he knocked loudly at
the door; he went in, related what had happened and talked
a little louder than he ought to have done. The judge began by fining him ten thousand piastres for the noise he had
made; he then listened patiently to him, promised to look
into his affair as soon as the merchant returned, and charged
him another ten thousand piastres for the expenses of the
audience.

This behavior reduced Candide to despair; he had indeed 130
endured misfortunes a thousand times more painful; but
the calmness of the judge and of the captain who had
robbed him, stirred up his bile and plunged him into a
black melancholy. The malevolence of men revealed itself
to his mind in all its ugliness; he entertained only gloomy
ideas.

At last a French ship was about to leave for Bordeaux and, since he no longer had any sheep laden with diamonds to put on board, he hired a cabin at a reasonable price and 140 announced throughout the town that he would give the passage, food and two thousand piastres to an honest man who would make the journey with him, on condition that this man was the most unfortunate and the most disgusted with his condition in the whole province. Such a crowd of applicants arrived that a fleet would not have contained them. Candide, wishing to choose among the most likely, picked out twenty persons who seemed reasonably sociable and who all claimed to deserve his preference. He collected them in a tavern and gave them supper, on condition that 150 each took an oath to relate truthfully the story of his life, promising that he would choose the man who seemed to him the most deserving of pity and to have the most cause for being discontented with his condition, and that he would give the others a little money. The sitting lasted until four o'clock in the morning. As Candide listened to their adventures he remembered what the old woman had said on the voyage to Buenos Ayres and how she had wagered that there was nobody on the boat who had not experienced very great misfortunes. At each story which was 160 told him, he thought of Pangloss.

"This Pangloss," said he, "would have some difficulty in supporting his system. I wish he were here. Certainly, if everything is well, it is only in Eldorado and not in the rest of the world."

He finally determined in favor of a poor man of letters who had worked ten years for the booksellers at Amsterdam. He judged that there was no occupation in the world which could more disgust a man.[3] This man of letters, who was also a good man, had been robbed by his wife, beaten 170 by his son, and abandoned by his daughter, who had eloped with a Portuguese. He had just been deprived of a small post on which he depended and the preachers of Surinam

3. **man** Voltaire had had unhappy personal dealings with the Dutch publishers.

were persecuting him because they thought he was a Socinian.[4] It must be admitted that the others were at least
as unfortunate as he was; but Candide hoped that this
learned man would help to pass the time during the voyage.
All his other rivals considered that Candide was doing them
a great injustice; but he soothed them down by giving each
of them a hundred piastres.

4. **Socinian** A sect resembling the Unitarians.

Chapter XX

WHAT HAPPENED TO CANDIDE AND MARTIN AT SEA

So the old man, who was called Martin, embarked with Candide for Bordeaux. Both had seen and suffered much; and if the ship had been sailing from Surinam to Japan by way of the Cape of Good Hope they would have been able to discuss moral and physical evil during the whole voyage. However, Candide had one great advantage over Martin, because he still hoped to see Mademoiselle Cunegonde again, and Martin had nothing to hope for; moreover, he possessed gold and diamonds; and, although he had lost a hundred
10 large red sheep laden with the greatest treasures on earth, although he was still enraged at being robbed by the Dutch captain, yet when he thought of what he still had left in his pockets and when he talked of Cunegonde, especially at the end of a meal, he still inclined towards the system of Pangloss.

"But what do you think of all this, Martin?" said he to the man of letters. "What is your view of moral and physical evil?"

"Sir," replied Martin, "my priests accused me of being
20 a Socinian; but the truth is I am a Manichean." [1]

"You are poking fun at me," said Candide, "there are no Manicheans left in the world."

"I am one," said Martin. "I don't know what to do about it, but I am unable to think in any other fashion."

"You must be possessed by the devil," said Candide.

1. **Manichean** A believer in the two Principles of Good and Evil which dispute the government of the universe and man's fate. The sect flourished at the time of St. Augustine.

"He takes so great a share in the affairs of this world," said Martin, "that he might well be in me, as he is everywhere else; but I confess that when I consider this globe, or rather this globule, I think that God has abandoned it to some evil creature—always excepting Eldorado. I have never seen a town which did not desire the ruin of the next town, never a family which did not wish to exterminate some other family. Everywhere the weak loathe the powerful before whom they cower and the powerful treat them like flocks of sheep whose wool and flesh are to be sold. A million drilled assassins go from one end of Europe to the other murdering and robbing with discipline in order to earn their bread, because there is no honester occupation; and in the towns which seem to enjoy peace and where the arts flourish, men are devoured by more envy, troubles and worries than the afflictions of a besieged town. Secret griefs are even more cruel than public miseries. In a word, I have seen so much and endured so much that I have become a Manichean."

"Yet there is some good," replied Candide.

"There may be," said Martin, "but I do not know it."

In the midst of this dispute they heard the sound of cannon. The noise increased every moment. Every one took his telescope. About three miles away they saw two ships engaged in battle; and the wind brought them so near the French ship that they had the pleasure [2] of seeing the fight at their ease. At last one of the two ships fired a broadside so accurately and so low down that the other ship began to sink. Candide and Martin distinctly saw a hundred men on the main deck of the sinking ship; they raised their hands to Heaven and uttered frightful shrieks; in a moment all were engulfed.

"Well!" said Martin, "that is how men treat each other."

"It is certainly true," said Candide, "that there is something diabolical in this affair."

As he was speaking, he saw something of a brilliant red

2. **pleasure** Ironical.

swimming near the ship. They launched a boat to see what it could be; it was one of his sheep. Candide felt more joy at recovering this sheep than grief at losing a hundred all laden with large diamonds from Eldorado.

The French captain soon perceived that the captain of the remaining ship was a Spaniard and that the sunken ship was a Dutch pirate; the captain was the very same who had robbed Candide. The immense wealth this scoundrel had 70 stolen was swallowed up with him in the sea and only a sheep was saved.

"You see," said Candide to Martin, "that crime is sometimes punished; this scoundrel of a Dutch captain has met the fate he deserved."

"Yes," said Martin, "but was it necessary that the other passengers on his ship should perish too? God punished the thief, and the devil punished the others."

Meanwhile the French and Spanish ships continued on their way and Candide continued his conversation with 80 Martin. They argued for a fortnight and at the end of the fortnight they had got no further than at the beginning. But after all, they talked, they exchanged ideas, they consoled each other. Candide stroked his sheep. "Since I have found you again," said he, "I may very likely find Cunegonde."

Chapter XXI

CANDIDE AND MARTIN APPROACH THE COAST OF FRANCE AND ARGUE

At last they sighted the coast of France.

"Have you ever been to France, Monsieur Martin?" said Candide.

"Yes," said Martin, "I have traversed several provinces. In some half the inhabitants are crazy, in others they are too artful, in some they are usually quite gentle and stupid, and in others they think they are clever; in all of them the chief occupation is making love, the second scandal-mongering and the third talking nonsense."

"But, Monsieur Martin, have you seen Paris?"   10

"Yes, I have seen Paris; it is a mixture of all the species; it is a chaos, a throng where everybody hunts for pleasure and hardly anybody finds it, at least so far as I could see. I did not stay there long; when I arrived there I was robbed of everything I had by pickpockets at Saint-Germain's fair; they thought I was a thief and I spent a week in prison; after which I became a printer's reader to earn enough to return to Holland on foot. I met the scribbling rabble, the intriguing rabble and the fanatical rabble. We hear that there are very polite people in the town; I am glad to   20 think so."

"For my part, I have not the least curiosity to see France," said Candide. "You can easily guess that when a man has spent a month in Eldorado he cares to see nothing else in the world but Mademoiselle Cunegonde. I shall go and wait for her at Venice; we will go to Italy by way of France; will you come with me?"

"Willingly," said Martin. "They say that Venice is only

for the Venetian nobles but that foreigners are nevertheless
30   well received when they have plenty of money; I have none,
you have plenty, I will follow you anywhere."

"Apropos," said Candide, "do you think the earth was
originally a sea, as we are assured by that large book [1] belonging to the captain?"

"I don't believe it in the least," said Martin, "any more
than all the other whimsies we have been pestered with
recently!"

"But to what end was this world formed?" said Candide.
"To infuriate us," replied Martin.

40   "Are you not very much surprised," continued Candide,
"by the love those two girls of the country of the Oreillons
had for those two monkeys, whose adventure I told you?"

"Not in the least," said Martin. "I see nothing strange in
their passion; I have seen so many extraordinary things that
nothing seems extraordinary to me."

"Do you think," said Candide, "that men have always
massacred each other, as they do today? Have they always
been liars, cheats, traitors, brigands, weak, flighty, cowardly,
envious, gluttonous, drunken, grasping, and vicious, bloody,
50   backbiting, debauched, fanatical, hypocritical and silly?"

"Do you think," said Martin, "that sparrow hawks have
always eaten the pigeons they came across?"

"Yes, of course," said Candide.

"Well," said Martin, "if sparrow hawks have always possessed the same nature, why should you expect men to
change theirs?"

"Oh!" said Candide, "there is a great difference; free
will . . ." Arguing thus, they arrived at Bordeaux.

1. **book** The large book might well be the Bible, or *The Theory of
the Earth* by Buffon, with whom Voltaire entered into more or less
friendly debate. The new geological ideas seemed at first to confirm
the Biblical flood.

Chapter XXII

WHAT HAPPENED TO CANDIDE AND MARTIN IN FRANCE

Candide remained in Bordeaux only long enough to sell a few Eldorado pebbles and to provide himself with a two-seated post chaise, for he could no longer get on without his philosopher Martin; but he was very much grieved at having to part with his sheep, which he left with the Academy of Sciences at Bordeaux. The Academy offered as the subject for a prize that year the cause of the redness of the sheep's fleece; and the prize was awarded to a learned man in the North, who proved by A plus B minus C divided by z that the sheep must be red and die of the sheep-pox. 10

However all the travellers Candide met in taverns on the way said to him: "We are going to Paris." This general eagerness at length made him wish to see that capital; it was not far out of the road to Venice.

He entered by the Faubourg Saint-Marceau[1] and thought he was in the ugliest village of Westphalia. Candide had scarcely reached his inn when he was attacked by a slight illness caused by fatigue. As he wore an enormous diamond on his finger, and a prodigiously heavy strongbox had been observed in his train, he immediately had with him two doc- 20 tors he had not asked for, several intimate friends who would not leave him and two devotees who kept making him broth.

Said Martin: "I remember that I was ill too when I first came to Paris; I was very poor; so I had no friends, no devotees, no doctors, and I got well."

1. **Saint-Marceau** In Voltaire's time, a dirty Parisian suburb. Voltaire wrote often in favor of the embellishment of Paris.

However, with the aid of medicine and bloodletting,[2] Candide's illness became serious. An inhabitant of the district came and gently asked him for a note payable to bearer in the next world;[3] Candide would have nothing to do with it. The devotees assured him that it was a new fashion; Candide replied that he was not a fashionable man. Martin wanted to throw the inhabitant out the window; the clerk swore that Candide should not be buried; Martin swore that he would bury the clerk if he continued to annoy them. The quarrel became heated; Martin took him by the shoulders and turned him out roughly; this caused a great scandal, and they made an official report on it.

Candide got better; and during his convalescence he had very good company to supper with him. They gambled for high stakes. Candide was vastly surprised that he never drew an ace; and Martin was not surprised at all.[4]

Among those who did the honors of the town was a little abbé from Périgord, one of those assiduous people who are always alert, always obliging, impudent, fawning, accommodating, always on the lookout for the arrival of foreigners, ready to tell them all the scandals of the town and to procure them pleasures at any price. This abbé took Candide and Martin to the theatre. A new tragedy was being played. Candide was seated near several wits. This did not prevent his weeping at perfectly played scenes. One of the argumentative bores near him said during an interval: "You have no business to weep, this is a very bad actress, the actor playing with her is still worse, the play is still worse than the actors; the author does not know a word of Arabic and yet the scene is in Arabia; moreover, he is a man who does

2. **bloodletting** An almost universal "remedy," from the Middle Ages to the eighteenth century.

3. **world** As a means of detecting their rivals, the Jansenists, the Jesuits in power required Parisians to carry proof that they had been to confession.

4. **all** Cheating at cards was a common practice, even at the court, as Voltaire knew from sad experience.

not believe in innate ideas;[5] tomorrow I will bring you twenty articles written against him."

"Sir," said Candide to the abbé, "how many plays have you in France?"

"Five or six thousand," he replied.

"That's a lot," said Candide, "and how many good ones are there?"

"Fifteen or sixteen," replied the other.

"That's a lot," said Martin.

Candide was greatly pleased with an actress who took the part of Queen Elizabeth in a rather dull tragedy which is sometimes played. "This actress," said he to Martin, "pleases me very much; she looks rather like Mademoiselle Cunegonde; I should be very glad to pay her my respects."

The abbé offered to introduce him to her. Candide, brought up in Germany, asked what was the etiquette, and how queens of England were treated in France.

"There is a distinction," said the abbé. "In the provinces we take them to a tavern; in Paris we respect them when they are beautiful and throw them in the public sewer when they are dead." [6]

"Queens in the public sewer!" said Candide.

"Yes, indeed," said Martin, "the abbé is right; I was in Paris when Mademoiselle Monime [7] departed, as they say, this life; she was refused what people here call the *honors of burial*—that is to say, the honor of rotting with all the beggars of the district in a horrible cemetery; she was buried by herself at the corner of the Rue de Bourgogne; which must have given her extreme pain, for her mind was very lofty."

"That was very impolite," said Candide.

"What do you expect?" said Martin. "These people are

5. **ideas** Descartes' philosophy was based on "innate ideas." Voltaire followed Locke in denying them.

6. **dead** Under the Old Regime, actors and actresses were refused burial in holy ground. Voltaire waged a strenuous and finally successful campaign against this discrimination.

7. **Monime** An actress (Adrienne Lecouvreur) whom Voltaire greatly admired and whom he helped to bury secretly at night.

like that. Imagine all possible contradictions and incom-
90 patibilities; you will see them in the government, in the law
courts, in the churches and the entertainments of this absurd
nation."

"Is it true that people are always laughing in Paris?" said
Candide.

"Yes," said the abbé, "but it is with rage in their hearts,
for they complain of everything with roars of laughter and
they even commit with laughter the most detestable ac-
tions."

"Who is that fat pig," said Candide, "who said so much
100 ill of the play I cried at so much and of the actors who gave
me so much pleasure?"

"He is a living evil," replied the abbé, "who earns his
living by abusing all plays and all books; he hates anyone
who succeeds, as eunuchs hate those who enjoy; he is one of
the serpents of literature who feed on filth and venom; he
is a scribbler."

"What do you mean by a scribbler?" said Candide.

"A scribbler of periodical sheets," said the abbé. "A
Fréron." [8]

110 Candide, Martin and the abbé from Périgord talked in
this manner on the stairway as they watched everybody going out after the play.

"Although I am most anxious to see Mademoiselle Cunegonde again," said Candide, "I should like to sup with
Mademoiselle Clairon,[9] for I thought her admirable."

The abbé was not the sort of man to know Mademoiselle
Clairon, for she saw only good company. "She is engaged
this evening," he said, "but I shall have the honor to take
you to the house of a lady of quality, and there you will
120 learn as much of Paris as if you had been here for four
years."

Candide, who was naturally curious, allowed himself to

8. **Fréron** The name of a successful journalist and critic who long
and insidiously attacked Voltaire.

9. **Clairon** A noted actress who was often leading lady in Voltaire's
plays.

be taken to the lady's house at the far end of the Faubourg
Saint-Honoré; [10] they were playing faro; twelve gloomy
punters [11] each held a small hand of cards, the foolish regis-
ter of their misfortunes. The silence was profound, the punters were pale, the banker was uneasy, and the lady of the
house, seated beside this pitiless banker, watched with lynx's
eyes every double stake, every seven-and-the-go, with which
each player marked his cards; she had them unmarked with   130
severe but polite attention, for fear of losing her customers;
the lady called herself Marquise de Parolignac. Her fifteen-
year-old daughter was among the punters and winked to
her to let her know the tricks of the poor people who attempted to repair the cruelties of fate. The abbé from Périgord, Candide and Martin entered; nobody rose, nobody
greeted them, nobody looked at them; every one was pro-
foundly occupied with the cards.

"Her Ladyship, the Baroness of Thunder-ten-tronckh was
more civil," said Candide.   140

However the abbé whispered in the ear of the Marquise,
who half rose, honored Candide with a gracious smile and
Martin with a most noble nod. Candide was given a seat
and a hand of cards, and lost fifty thousand francs in two
hands; after which they supped very merrily and everyone
was surprised that Candide was not more disturbed by his
loss. The lackeys said to each other, in the language of
lackeys: "He must be an English Milord."

The supper was like most suppers in Paris; first there was
a silence and then a noise of indistinguishable words, then   150
jokes, most of which were insipid, false news, false arguments, some politics and a great deal of scandal; there was
even some talk of new books.

"Have you seen," said the abbé from Périgord, "the
novel by Gauchat,[12] the doctor of theology?"

"Yes," replied one of the guests, "but I could not finish it.
We have a crowd of silly writings, but all of them together

10. **Saint-Honoré** A wealthy, aristocratic section of Paris.
11. **punters** Those who bet against the banker.
12. **Gauchat** Another enemy of Voltaire and the Encyclopedists.

do not approach the silliness of Gauchat, doctor of theology. I am so weary of this immensity of detestable books which
160 inundates us that I have taken to faro."

"And what do you say about the *Mélanges* by Archdeacon Trublet?" said the abbé. "Ah!" said Madame de Parolignac, "the tiresome creature! How carefully he tells you what everybody knows! How heavily he discusses what is not worth the trouble of being lightly mentioned! How witlessly he appropriates other people's wit! How he spoils what he steals! How he disgusts me! But he will not disgust me any more; it is enough to have read a few pages by the Archdeacon."

170 There was a man of learning and taste at table who confirmed what the marchioness had said. They then talked of tragedies; the lady asked why there were tragedies which were sometimes played and yet were unreadable. The man of taste explained very clearly how a play might have some interest and hardly any merit; in a few words he proved that it was not sufficient to bring in one or two of the situations which are found in all novels and which always attract the spectators; but that a writer of tragedies must be original without being bizarre, often sublime and always
180 natural, must know the human heart and be able to give it speech, must be a great poet but not let any character in his play appear to be a poet, must know his language perfectly, speak it with purity, with continual harmony and never allow the sense to be spoilt for the sake of the rhyme.

"Anyone," he added, "who does not observe all these rules may produce one or two tragedies applauded in the theatre, but he will never be ranked among good writers; there are very few good tragedies; some are idylls in well-written and well-rhymed dialogue; some are political arguments which
190 send one to sleep, or repulsive amplifications; others are the dreams of an enthusiast, in a barbarous style, with broken dialogue, long apostrophes to the gods (because he does not know how to speak to men), false maxims and turgid commonplaces."

Candide listened attentively to these remarks and con-

ceived a great idea of the speaker; and, as the marchioness
had been careful to place him beside her, he leaned over to
her ear and took the liberty of asking her who was the man
who talked so well.

"He is a man of letters," said the lady, "who does not   200
play cards and is sometimes brought here to supper by the
abbé; he has a perfect knowledge of tragedies and books
and he has written a tragedy which was hissed and a book
of which only one copy has ever been seen outside his
bookseller's shop and that was one he gave me."

"The great man!" said Candide. "He is another Pangloss."

Then, turning to him, Candide said: "Sir, no doubt you
think that all is for the best in the physical world and in the
moral, and that nothing could be otherwise than as it is?"   210

"Sir," replied the man of letters, "I do not think anything
of the sort. I think everything goes awry with us, that nobody knows his rank or his office, nor what he is doing,
nor what he ought to do, and that except at supper, which
is quite gay and where there appears to be a certain amount
of sociability, all the rest of their time is passed in senseless
quarrels: Jansenists with Molinists,[13] lawyers with church-
men, men of letters with men of letters, courtiers with courtiers, financiers with the people, wives with husbands,
relatives with relatives—'tis an eternal war."   220

Candide replied: "I have seen worse things; but a wise
man, who has since had the misfortune to be hanged, taught
me that it is all for the best; these are only the shadows in
a fair picture."

"Your wise man who was hanged was poking fun at the
world," said Martin; "and your shadows are horrible stains."

"The stains are made by men," said Candide, "and they
cannot avoid them."

"Then it is not their fault," said Martin.

Most of the gamblers, who had not the slightest under-   230
standing of this kind of talk, were drinking; Martin argued

13. **Molinists** Synonym for Jesuits. Molina, a member of the order,
was an authority used against the Jansenist heresy.

with the man of letters and Candide told the hostess some
of his adventures.

After supper the marchioness took Candide into a side
room and made him sit down on a sofa.

"Well!" said she, "so you are still madly in love with
Mademoiselle Cunegonde of Thunder-ten-tronckh?"

"Yes, madame," replied Candide.

The marchioness replied with a tender smile: "You an-
240 swer like a young man from Westphalia. A Frenchman
would have said: 'It is true that I was in love with Mademoiselle Cunegonde, but when I see you, madame, I fear
lest I should cease to love her.'"

"Alas! madame," said Candide, "I will answer as you
wish."

"Your passion for her," said the marchioness, "began by
picking up her handkerchief; I want you to pick up my
garter."

"With all my heart," said Candide; and he picked it up.
250 "But I want you to put it on again," said the lady; and
Candide put it on again.

"You see," said the lady, "you are a foreigner; I sometimes make my lovers in Paris languish for a fortnight, but
I give myself to you the very first night, because one must
do the honors of one's country to a young man from Westphalia."

The fair lady, having perceived two enormous diamonds
on the young foreigner's hands, praised them so sincerely
that they passed from Candide's fingers to the fingers of
260 the marchioness. As Candide went home with his abbé from
Périgord, he felt some remorse at having been unfaithful to
Mademoiselle Cunegonde. The abbé sympathised with his
distress; he had only had a small share in the fifty thousand
francs Candide had lost at cards and in the value of the
two half-given, half-extorted, diamonds. His plan was to
profit as much as he could from the advantages which his
acquaintance with Candide might procure for him. He
talked a lot about Cunegonde and Candide told him that
he should ask that fair one's forgiveness for his infidelity

when he saw her at Venice. The abbé from Périgord re- 270
doubled his politeness and civilities and took a tender interest in all Candide said, in all he did, and in all he wished
to do.

"Then, sir," said he, "you are to meet her at Venice?"

"Yes, sir," said Candide, "without fail I must go and
meet Mademoiselle Cunegonde there."

Then, carried away by the pleasure of talking about the
person he loved, he related, as he was accustomed to do,
some of his adventures with that illustrious Westphalian
lady. 280

"I suppose," said the abbé, "that Mademoiselle Cunegonde has a great deal of wit and that she writes charming
letters."

"I have never received any from her," said Candide, "for
you must know that when I was expelled from the castle
because of my love for her, I could not write to her; soon
afterwards I heard she was dead, then I found her again
and then I lost her, and now I have sent an express messen-
ger to her two thousand five hundred leagues from here and
am expecting her reply." 290

The abbé listened attentively and seemed rather medi-
tative. He soon took leave of the two foreigners, after having embraced them tenderly.

The next morning when Candide woke up he received
a letter composed as follows: "Sir, my dearest lover, I have
been ill for a week in this town; I have just heard that you
are here. I should fly to your arms if I could stir. I heard
that you had passed through Bordeaux; I left the faithful
Cacambo and the old woman there and they will soon follow me. The governor of Buenos Ayres took everything, 300
but I still have your heart. Come, your presence will restore
me to life or will make me die of pleasure."

This charming, this unhoped-for letter, transported Candide with inexpressible joy; and the illness of his dear
Cunegonde overwhelmed him with grief. Torn between
these two sentiments, he took his gold and his diamonds
and drove with Martin to the hotel where Mademoiselle

Cunegonde was staying. He entered trembling with emotion, his heart beat, his voice was broken; he wanted to
310 open the bed curtains and to have a light brought.

"Do nothing of the sort," said the waitingmaid. "Light would be the death of her." And she quickly drew the curtains.

"My dear Cunegonde," said Candide, weeping, "how do you feel? If you cannot see me, at least speak to me."

"She cannot speak," said the maidservant.

The lady then extended a plump hand, which Candide watered with his tears and then filled with diamonds, leaving a bag full of gold in the armchair. In the midst of these
320 transports a police officer arrived, followed by the abbé from Périgord and a squad of policemen.

"So these are the two suspicious foreigners?" he said.

He had them arrested immediately and ordered his bravoes to hale them off to prison.

"This is not the way they treat travellers in Eldorado," said Candide.

"I am more of a Manichean than ever," said Martin.

"But, sir, where are you taking us?" said Candide.

"To the deepest dungeon," said the police officer.

330 Martin, having recovered his coolness, decided that the lady who pretended to be Cunegonde was a cheat, that the abbé from Périgord was a cheat who had abused Candide's innocence with all possible speed, and that the police officer was another cheat of whom they could easily be rid. Rather than expose himself to judicial proceedings, Candide, enlightened by this advice and impatient to see the real Cunegonde again, offered the police officer three little diamonds worth about three thousand pounds each.

"Ah! sir," said the man with the ivory stick, "if you had
340 committed all imaginable crimes you would be the most honest man in the world. Three diamonds! Each worth three thousand pounds each! Sir! I would be killed for your sake, instead of taking you to prison. All strangers are arrested here, but trust to me. I have a brother at Dieppe in Normandy, I will take you there; and if you have any dia-

monds to give him he will take as much care of you as my-self."

"And why are all strangers arrested?" said Candide.

The abbé from Périgord then spoke and said: "It is be-cause a scoundrel from Atrebatum [14] listened to imbecilities; 350 this alone made him commit a parricide, not like that of May 1610, but like that of December 1594,[15] and like sev-eral others committed in other years and in other months by other scoundrels who had listened to imbecilities."

The police officer then explained what it was all about.

"Ah! the monsters!" cried Candide. "What! Can such horrors be in a nation which dances and sings! Can I not leave at once this country where monkeys torment tigers? I have seen bears in my own country; Eldorado is the only place where I have seen men. In God's name, sir, take me 360 to Venice, where I am to wait for Mademoiselle Cune-gonde."

"I can only take you to Lower Normandy," said the barigel.[16]

Immediately he took off their irons, said there had been a mistake, sent his men away, took Candide and Martin to Dieppe, and left them with his brother. There was a small Dutch vessel in the port. With the help of three other dia-monds the Norman became the most obliging of men and embarked Candide and his servants in the ship which was 370 about to sail for Portsmouth in England. It was not the road to Venice; but Candide felt as if he had escaped from Hell, and he had every intention of taking the road to Venice at the first opportunity.

14. Atrebatum Latin name for the region around Arras, the home of Damiens, who attempted to stab Louis XV in 1757.

15. 1594 In 1610, Ravaillac assassinated Henry IV, after Châtel's earlier attempt in 1594 had failed.

16. barigel Police officer.

Chapter XXIII

CANDIDE AND MARTIN REACH THE COAST OF ENGLAND; AND WHAT THEY SAW THERE

"Ah! Pangloss, Pangloss! Ah! Martin, Martin! Ah! my dear Cunegonde! What sort of a world is this?" said Candide on the Dutch ship.

"Something very mad and very abominable," replied Martin.

"You know England; are the people there as mad as they are in France?"

" 'Tis another sort of madness," said Martin. "You know these two nations are at war for a few acres of snow in
10 Canada, and that they are spending more on this fine war than all Canada is worth.[1] It is beyond my poor capacity to tell you whether there are more madmen in one country than in the other; all I know is that in general the people we are going to visit are extremely melancholic."[2]

Talking thus, they arrived at Portsmouth. There were multitudes of people on the shore, looking attentively at a rather fat man who was kneeling down with his eyes bandaged on the deck of one of the ships in the fleet; four soldiers placed opposite this man each shot three bullets into
20 his brain in the calmest manner imaginable; and the whole assembly returned home with great satisfaction.

"What is all this?" said Candide. "And what Demon ex-

1. **worth** Voltaire favored the French colonies in Louisiana and the West Indies at the expense of Canada, which was more under Jesuit control.

2. **melancholic** Voltaire believed the cause of this national trait was England's east wind.

ercises his power everywhere?" He asked who was the fat
man who had just been killed so ceremoniously.

"An admiral," was the reply.

"And why kill the admiral?"

"Because," he was told, "he did not kill enough people.
He fought a battle with a French admiral and it was held
that the English admiral was not close enough to him."

"But," said Candide, "the French admiral was just as 30
far from the English admiral!"

"That is indisputable," was the answer, "but in this country it is a good thing to kill an admiral from time to time
to encourage the others." [3]

Candide was so bewildered and so shocked by what he
saw and heard that he would not even set foot on shore, but
bargained with the Dutch captain (even if he had to pay
him as much as the Surinam robber) to take him at once to
Venice. The captain was ready in two days. They sailed
down the coast of France; and passed in sight of Lisbon, at 40
which Candide shuddered. They entered the Straits and the
Mediterranean and at last reached Venice. "Praised be God!"
said Candide, embracing Martin, "here I shall see the fair
Cunegonde again. I trust Cacambo as I would myself. All
is well, all goes well, all goes as well as it possibly could."

3. Voltaire had tried by every means in his command to secure a
reprieve for Admiral Byng, executed in 1757. This ironical shaft con-
ceals his bitterness over his failure to obtain justice.

Chapter XXIV

PAQUETTE AND FRIAR GIROFLÉE

As soon as he reached Venice, he inquired for Cacambo in all the taverns, in all the cafés, and of all the ladies of pleasure; and did not find him. Every day he sent out messengers to all ships and boats; but there was no news of Cacambo. "What!" said he to Martin, "I have had time to sail from Surinam to Bordeaux, to go from Bordeaux to Paris, from Paris to Dieppe, from Dieppe to Portsmouth, to sail along the coasts of Portugal and Spain, to cross the Mediterranean, to spend several months at Venice, and the fair
10 Cunegonde has not yet arrived! Instead of her I have met only a jade and an abbé from Périgord! Cunegonde is certainly dead and the only thing left for me is to die too. Ah! It would have been better to stay in the Paradise of Eldorado instead of returning to this accursed Europe. How right you are, my dear Martin! Everything is illusion and calamity!"

He fell into a black melancholy and took no part in the opera *à la mode* or in the other carnival amusements; not a lady caused him the least temptation.

20 Martin said: "You are indeed simple-minded to suppose that a half-breed valet with five or six millions in his pocket will go and look for your mistress at the other end of the world and bring her to you at Venice. If he finds her, he will take her for himself; if he does not find her, he will take another. I advise you to forget your valet Cacambo and your mistress Cunegonde."

Martin was not consoling. Candide's melancholy increased, and Martin persisted in proving to him that there was little

virtue and small happiness in the world except perhaps in
Eldorado where nobody could go.   30

While arguing about this important subject and waiting
for Cunegonde, Candide noticed a young Theatine [1] monk
in the Piazza San Marco,[2] with a girl on his arm. The
Theatine looked fresh, plump and vigorous; his eyes were
bright, his air assured, his countenance firm, and his step
lofty. The girl was very pretty and was singing; she gazed
amorously at her Theatine and every now and then pinched
his fat cheeks.

"At least you will admit," said Candide to Martin, "that
those people are happy. Hitherto I have only found un-   40
fortunates in the whole habitable earth, except in Eldorado;
but I wager that this girl and the Theatine are very happy
creatures."

"I wager they are not," said Martin.

"We have only to ask them to dinner," said Candide,
"and you will see whether I am wrong."

He immediately accosted them, paid his respects to them,
and invited them to come to his hotel to eat macaroni, Lom-
bardy partridges, and caviare, and to drink Montepulciano,
Lacryma Christi, Cyprus and Samos wine. The young lady   50
blushed, the Theatine accepted the invitation, and the girl
followed, looking at Candide with surprise and confusion in
her eyes which were filled with a few tears. Scarcely had
they entered Candide's room when she said: "What! Monsieur Candide does not recognise Paquette!"

At these words Candide, who had not looked at her very
closely because he was occupied entirely by Cunegonde, said
to her: "Alas! my poor child, so it was you who put Dr.
Pangloss into the fine state I saw him in?"

"Alas! sir, it was indeed," said Paquette. "I see you have 60
heard all about it. I have heard of the terrible misfortunes
which happened to Her Ladyship the Baroness's whole family and to the fair Cunegonde. I swear to you that my fate
has been just as sad. I was very innocent when you knew me.

1. Theatine A Catholic order formed in 1524.
2. Marco The most famous square in Venice.

A Franciscan friar who was my confessor easily seduced me. The results were dreadful; I was obliged to leave the castle shortly after His Lordship the Baron expelled you by kicking you hard and frequently in the backside. If a famous doctor had not taken pity on me I should have died. For 70 some time I was the doctor's mistress from gratitude to him. His wife, who was madly jealous, beat me every day relentlessly; she was a fury. The doctor was the ugliest of men, and I was the most unhappy of all living creatures at being continually beaten on account of a man I did not love. You know, sir, how dangerous it is for a shrewish woman to be the wife of a doctor. One day, exasperated by his wife's behavior, he gave her some medicine for a little cold and it was so efficacious that she died two hours afterwards in horrible convulsions. The lady's relatives brought a criminal 80 prosecution against the husband; he fled and I was put in prison. My innocence would not have saved me if I had not been rather pretty. The judge set me free on condition that he took the doctor's place. I was soon supplanted by a rival, expelled without a penny, and obliged to continue the abominable occupation which to you men seems so amusing and which to us is nothing but an abyss of misery. I came to Venice to practise this profession. Ah! sir, if you could imagine what it is to be forced to caress impartially an old tradesman, a lawyer, a monk, a gondolier, an abbé; to be 90 exposed to every insult and outrage; to be reduced often to borrow a petticoat in order to go and find some disgusting man who will lift it; to be robbed by one of what one has earned with another, to be despoiled by the police, and to contemplate for the future nothing but a dreadful old age, a hospital and a dunghill, you would conclude that I am one of the most unfortunate creatures in the world."

Paquette opened her heart in this way to Candide in a side room, in the presence of Martin, who said to Candide: "You see, I have already won half my wager."

100 Friar Giroflée had remained in the dining room, drinking a glass while he waited for dinner.

"But," said Candide to Paquette, "when I met you, you

looked so gay, so happy; you were singing, you were caressing the Theatine so naturally; you seemed to me to be as happy as you are unfortunate."

"Ah! sir," replied Paquette, "that is one more misery of our profession. Yesterday I was robbed and beaten by an officer, and today I must seem to be in a good humor to please a monk."

Candide wanted to hear no more; he admitted that Martin was right. They sat down to table with Paquette and the Theatine. The meal was quite amusing and towards the end they were talking with some confidence.

"Father," said Candide to the monk, "you seem to me to enjoy a fate which everybody should envy; the flower of health shines on your cheek, your face is radiant with happiness; you have a very pretty girl for your recreation and you appear to be very well pleased with your state of life as a Theatine."

"Faith, Sir," said Friar Giroflée, "I wish all the Theatines were at the bottom of the sea. A hundred times I have been tempted to set fire to the monastery and to go and be a Turk. My parents forced me at the age of fifteen to put on this detestable robe,[3] in order that more money might be left to my cursed elder brother, whom God confound! Jealousy, discord, fury, inhabit the monastery. It is true, I have preached a few bad sermons which bring me in a little money, half of which is stolen from me by the prior; the remainder I spend on girls; but when I go back to the monastery in the evening I feel ready to smash my head against the dormitory walls, and all my colleagues are in the same state."

Martin turned to Candide and said with his usual calm: "Well, have I not won the whole wager?"

Candide gave two thousand piastres to Paquette and a thousand to Friar Giroflée. "I warrant," said he, "that they will be happy with that."

"I don't believe it in the very least," said Martin. "Perhaps

3. **robe** Forced vows were common and constituted one of the greatest abuses of the Old Regime.

you will make them still more unhappy with those piastres."

140 "That may be," said Candide, "but I am consoled by one thing; I see that we often meet people we thought we should never meet again; it may very well be that as I met my red sheep and Paquette, I may also meet Cunegonde again."

"I hope," said Martin, "that she will one day make you happy; but I doubt it very much."

"You are very hard," said Candide.

"That's because I have lived," said Martin.

"But look at these gondoliers," said Candide, "they sing
150 all day long."

"You do not see them at home, with their wives and their brats of children," said Martin. "The Doge has his troubles, the gondoliers have theirs. True, looking at it all round, a gondolier's lot is preferable to a Doge's; but I think the difference so slight that it is not worth examining."

"They talk," said Candide, "about Senator Pococurante [4] who lives in that handsome palace on the Brenta and who is hospitable to foreigners. He is supposed to be a man who has never known a grief."

160 "I should like to meet so rare a specimen," said Martin.

Candide immediately sent a request to Lord Pococurante for permission to wait upon him next day.

4. Pococurante The name ("caring little," in Italian) suggests the indifference and boredom of its bearer.

Chapter XXV

VISIT TO THE NOBLE VENETIAN, LORD POCOCURANTE

Candide and Martin took a gondola and rowed to the noble Pococurante's palace. The gardens were extensive and ornamented with fine marble statues; the architecture of the palace was handsome. The master of this establishment, a very wealthy man of about sixty, received the two visitors very politely but with very little cordiality, which disconcerted Candide but did not displease Martin. Two pretty and neatly dressed girls served them with very frothy chocolate. Candide could not refrain from praising their beauty, their grace and their skill. 10

"They are quite good creatures," said Senator Pococurante, "and I sometimes make them sleep in my bed, for I am very tired of the ladies of the town, with their coquetries, their jealousies, their quarrels, their humors, their meanness, their pride, their folly, and the sonnets one must write or have written for them; but, after all, I am getting very tired of these two girls."

After this collation, Candide was walking in a long gallery and was surprised by the beauty of the pictures. He asked what master had painted the two first. 20

"They are by Raphael," said the Senator. "Some years ago I bought them at a very high price out of mere vanity; I am told they are the finest in Italy, but they give me no pleasure; the color has gone very dark, the faces are not sufficiently rounded and do not stand out enough; the draperies have not the least resemblance to material; in short, whatever they may say, I do not consider them a true imi-

tation of nature. I shall only like a picture when it makes
me think it is nature itself; and there are none of that kind.
30 I have a great many pictures, but I never look at them now."

While they waited for dinner, Pococurante gave them a
concert. Candide thought the music delicious.

"This noise," said Pococurante, "is amusing for half an
hour; but if it lasts any longer, it wearies everybody although nobody dares to say so. Music nowadays is merely
the art of executing difficulties and in the end that which is
only difficult ceases to please. Perhaps I should like the opera
more, if they had not made it a monster which revolts me.
Those who please may go to see bad tragedies set to music,
40 where the scenes are only composed to bring in clumsily two
or three ridiculous songs which show off an actress's voice;
those who will or can, may swoon with pleasure when they
see an eunuch humming the part of Cæsar and Cato as he
awkwardly treads the boards; for my part, I long ago abandoned such trivialities, which nowadays are the glory of
Italy and for which monarchs pay so dearly."

Candide demurred a little, but discreetly. Martin entirely
agreed with the Senator.

They sat down to table and after an excellent dinner went
50 into the library. Candide saw a magnificently bound Homer
and complimented the Illustrissimo on his good taste. "That
is the book," said he, "which so much delighted the great
Pangloss, the greatest philosopher of Germany."

"It does not delight me," said Pococurante coldly; "formerly I was made to believe that I took pleasure in reading
it; but this continual repetition of battles which are all alike,
these gods who are perpetually active and achieve nothing
decisive, this Helen who is the cause of the war and yet
scarcely an actor in the piece, this Troy which is always be-
60 sieged and never taken—all bore me extremely. I have
sometimes asked learned men if they were as bored as I am
by reading it; all who were sincere confessed that the book
fell from their hands, but that it must be in every library,
as a monument of antiquity, and like those rusty coins
which cannot be put into circulation."

"Your Excellency has a different opinion of Virgil?"[1]
said Candide.

"I admit," said Pococurante, "that the second, fourth and
sixth books of his Æneid are excellent, but as for his pious
Æneas and the strong Cloanthes and the faithful Achates   70
and the little Ascanius and the imbecile king Latinus and
the middle-class Amata and the insipid Lavinia, I think
there could be nothing more frigid and disagreeable. I prefer Tasso and the fantastic tales of Ariosto."[2]

"May I venture to ask you, sir," said Candide, "if you do
not take great pleasure in reading Horace?"

"He has some maxims," said Pococurante, "which might
be useful to a man of the world, and which, being com-
pressed in energetic verses, are more easily impressed upon
the memory; but I care very little for his Journey to Brund- 80
isium, and his description of a Bad Dinner, and the street
brawlers' quarrel between—what is his name?—Rupilius,
whose words, he says, were full of pus, and another person
whose words were all vinegar.[3] I was extremely disgusted
with his gross verses against old women and witches; and
I cannot see there is any merit in his telling his friend
Mæcenas that, if he is placed by him among the lyric poets,
he will strike the stars with his lofty brow. Fools admire
everything in a celebrated author. I only read to please myself, and I only like what suits me."   90

Candide, who had been taught never to judge anything
for himself, was greatly surprised by what he heard; and
Martin thought Pococurante's way of thinking quite reasonable.

"Oh! There is a Cicero," said Candide. "I suppose you
are never tired of reading that great man?"

"I never read him," replied the Venetian. "What do I
care that he pleaded for Rabirius or Cluentius. I have

1. **Virgil** Placed generally by critics above Homer, until the nine-
teenth century.

2. **Ariosto** Voltaire himself was especially fond of Tasso's *Jerusalem
Delivered* and Ariosto's *Roland (Orlando furioso)*.

3. **vinegar** Eighteenth-century taste was finical and could not toler-
ate such "low" words.

enough cases to judge myself; I could better have endured
100 his philosophical works; but when I saw that he doubted
everything, I concluded I knew as much as he and did not
need anybody else in order to be ignorant."

"Ah! There are eighty volumes of the Proceedings of an
Academy of Sciences," exclaimed Martin, "there might be
something good in them."

"There would be," said Pococurante, "if a single one of
the authors of all that rubbish had invented even the art of
making pins; but in all those books there is nothing but
vain systems and not a single useful thing."

110 "What a lot of plays I see there," said Candide. "Italian,
Spanish, and French!"

"Yes," said the Senator, "there are three thousand and not
three dozen good ones. As for those collections of sermons,
which all together are not worth a page of Seneca, and all
those large volumes of theology you may well suppose that
they are never opened by me or anybody else."

Martin noticed some shelves filled with English books. "I
should think," he said, "that a republican would enjoy most
of those works written with so much freedom." [4]

120 "Yes," replied Pococurante, "it is good to write as we
think; it is the privilege of man. In all Italy, we only write
what we do not think; those who inhabit the country of
the Cæsars and the Antonines dare not have an idea without
the permission of a Dominican monk. I should applaud the
liberty which inspires Englishmen of genius if passion and
party spirit did not corrupt everything estimable in that
precious liberty."

Candide, in noticing a Milton, asked him if he did not
consider that author to be a very great man.

130 "Who?" said Pococurante. "That barbarian who wrote a
long commentary on the first chapter of Genesis in ten
books of harsh verses? That gross imitator of the Greeks,
who disfigures the Creation, and who, while Moses repre-
sents the Eternal Being as producing the world by speech,

4. **freedom** England enjoyed great freedom of thought compared
with the strict censorship in France.

makes the Messiah take a large compass from the heavenly
cupboard in order to trace out his work? Should I esteem
the man who spoiled Tasso's hell and devil; who disguises
Lucifer sometimes as a toad, sometimes as a pigmy; who
makes him repeat the same things a hundred times; makes
him argue about theology; and imitates seriously Ariosto's   140
comical invention of firearms by making the devils fire a
cannon in Heaven? Neither I nor anyone else in Italy could
enjoy such wretched extravagances. The marriage of Sin
and Death and the snakes which sin brings forth nauseate
any man of delicate taste, and his long description of a hospital would only please a gravedigger. This obscure, bizarre
and disgusting poem was despised at its birth; I treat it today as it was treated by its contemporaries in its own country. But then I say what I think, and care very little whether
others think as I do."   150

Candide was distressed by these remarks; he respected
Homer and rather liked Milton.[5]

"Alas!" he whispered to Martin, "I am afraid this man
would have a sovereign contempt for our German poets."

"There wouldn't be much harm in that," said Martin.

"Oh! What a superior man!" said Candide under his
breath. "What a great genius this Pococurante is! Nothing
can please him."

After they had thus reviewed all his books they went
down into the garden. Candide praised all its beauties.   160

"I have never met anything more tasteless," said the
owner. "We have nothing but gewgaws; but tomorrow I
shall begin to plant one on a more noble plan."

When the two visitors had taken farewell of his Excellency, Candide said to Martin: "Now you will admit that
he is the happiest of men, for he is superior to everything
he possesses."

"Do you not see," said Martin, "that he is disgusted with
everything he possesses? Plato said long ago that the best
stomachs are not those which refuse all food."   170

5. Milton Voltaire, too, rather liked Milton, in spite of his "flaws."

"But," said Candide, "is there not pleasure in criticising, in finding faults where other men think they see beauty?"

"That is to say," answered Martin, "that there is pleasure in not being pleased."

"Oh! Well," said Candide, "then there is no one happy except me—when I see Mademoiselle Cunegonde again."

"It is always good to hope," said Martin.

However, the days and weeks went by; Cacambo did not return and Candide was so much plunged in grief that he 180 did not even notice that Paquette and Friar Giroflée had not once come to thank him.

Chapter XXVI

HOW CANDIDE AND MARTIN SUPPED
WITH SIX STRANGERS AND
WHO THEY WERE

One evening when Candide and Martin were going to sit down to table with the strangers who lodged in the same hotel, a man with a face the color of soot came up to him from behind and, taking him by the arm, said: "Get ready to come with us, and do not fail."

He turned round and saw Cacambo. Only the sight of Cunegonde could have surprised and pleased him more. He was almost wild with joy. He embraced his dear friend.

"Cunegonde is here, of course? Where is she? Take me to her, let me die of joy with her." 10

"Cunegonde is not here," said Cacambo. "She is in Constantinople."

"Heavens! In Constantinople! But, were she in China, I would fly to her; let us start at once."

"We will start after supper," replied Cacambo. "I cannot tell you any more; I am a slave, and my master is waiting for me; I must go and serve him at table! Do not say anything; eat your supper, and be in readiness."

Candide, torn between joy and grief, charmed to see his faithful agent again, amazed to see him a slave, filled with 20 the idea of seeing his mistress again, with turmoil in his heart, agitation in his mind, sat down to table with Martin (who met every strange occurrence with the same calmness), and with six strangers, who had come to spend the Carnival at Venice.

Cacambo, who acted as butler to one of the strangers,

bent down to his master's head towards the end of the meal and said: "Sire, your Majesty can leave when you wish, the ship is ready." After saying this, Cacambo withdrew.

30 The guests looked at each other with surprise without saying a word, when another servant came up to his master and said: "Sire, your Majesty's post chaise is at Padua, and the boat is ready." The master made a sign and the servant departed.

Once more all the guests looked at each other, and the general surprise was increased twofold. A third servant went up to the third stranger and said: "Sire, believe me, your Majesty cannot remain here any longer; I will prepare everything." And he immediately disappeared.

40 Candide and Martin had no doubt that this was a Carnival masquerade. A fourth servant said to the fourth master: "Your Majesty can leave when you wish." And he went out like the others. The fifth servant spoke similarly to the fifth master. But the sixth servant spoke differently to the sixth stranger who was next to Candide, and said: "Faith, sire, they will not give your Majesty any more credit nor me either, and we may very likely be jailed tonight, both of us; I am going to look to my own affairs, good bye."

When the servants had all gone, the six strangers, Can-
50 dide and Martin remained in profound silence. At last it was broken by Candide.

"Gentlemen," said he, "this is a curious jest. How is it you are all kings? I confess that neither Martin nor I are kings."

Cacambo's master then gravely spoke and said in Italian: "I am not jesting, my name is Achmet III. For several years I was Sultan; I dethroned my brother; my nephew dethroned me; they cut off the heads of my viziers; I am ending my days in the old seraglio; my nephew, Sultan Mahmoud,
50 sometimes allows me to travel for my health, and I have come to spend the Carnival at Venice."

A young man who sat next to Achmet spoke after him and said: "My name is Ivan; I was Emperor of all the Russias; I was dethroned in my cradle; [1] my father and mother were imprisoned and I was brought up in prison; I sometimes have permission to travel, accompanied by those who guard me, and I have come to spend the Carnival at Venice."

The third said: "I am Charles Edward, King of England; [2] my father gave up his rights to the throne to me and I fought a war to assert them; the hearts of eight hundred of my adherents were torn out and dashed in their faces. I have been in prison; I am going to Rome to visit the King, my father, who is dethroned like my grandfather and me; and I have come to spend the Carnival at Venice."

The fourth then spoke and said: "I am the King of Poland; the chance of war deprived me of my hereditary states; my father endured the same reverse of fortune; I am resigned to Providence like the Sultan Achmet, the Emperor Ivan and King Charles Edward, to whom God grant long life; and I have come to spend the Carnival at Venice."

The fifth said: "I also am the King of Poland, [3] I have lost my kingdom twice; but Providence has given me another state in which I have been able to do more good than all the kings of the Sarmatians together have been ever able to do on the banks of the Vistula; I also am resigned to Providence and I have come to spend the Carnival at Venice."

It was now for the sixth monarch to speak. "Gentlemen," said he, "I am not so eminent as you; but I have been a king like anyone else. I am Theodore; I was elected King of Corsica; I have been called Your Majesty and now I am barely called Sir. I have coined money and do not own a farthing; I have had two Secretaries of State and now have scarcely a valet; I have occupied a throne and for a long time lay on straw in a London prison. I am much afraid I

1. **cradle** Ivan IV, dethroned in 1741, before he was two years old. All these kings are genuine.
2. **England** The "Young Pretender," son of James Stuart.
3. **Poland** Stanislas Leczinski, father-in-law of the French king, Louis XV. He became Duke of Lorraine and befriended Voltaire.

shall be treated in the same way here, although I have come, like your Majesties, to spend the Carnival at Venice."

100 The five other kings listened to this speech with a noble compassion. Each of them gave King Theodore twenty sequins [4] to buy clothes and shirts; Candide presented him with a diamond worth two thousand sequins.

"Who is this man," said the five kings, "who is able to give a hundred times as much as any of us, and who gives it?"

As they were leaving the table, there came to the same hotel four serene highnesses who had also lost their states in the chance of war, and who had come to spend the rest of the Carnival at Venice; but Candide did not even notice 110 these newcomers, he could think of nothing but of going to Constantinople to find his dear Cunegonde.

4. sequins Gold coin of Venice.

Chapter XXVII

CANDIDE'S VOYAGE TO CONSTANTINOPLE

The faithful Cacambo had already spoken to the Turkish captain who was to take Sultan Achmet back to Constantinople and had obtained permission for Candide and Martin to come on board. They both entered this ship after having prostrated themselves before his miserable Highness.

On the way, Candide said to Martin: "So we have just supped with six dethroned kings! And among those six kings there was one to whom I gave charity. Perhaps there are many other princes still more unfortunate. Now, I have only lost a hundred sheep and I am hastening to Cunegonde's arms. My dear Martin, once more, Pangloss was right, all is well."

"I hope so," said Martin.

"But," said Candide, "this is a very singular experience we have just had at Venice. Nobody has ever seen or heard of six dethroned kings supping together in a tavern."

" 'Tis no more extraordinary," said Martin, "than most of the things which have happened to us. It is very common for kings to be dethroned; and as to the honor we have had of supping with them, 'tis a trifle not deserving our attention."

Scarcely had Candide entered the ship when he threw his arms round the neck of his old valet, of his friend Cacambo.

"Well!" said he, "what is Cunegonde doing? Is she still a marvel of beauty? Does she still love me? How is she? Of course you have bought her a palace in Constantinople?"

"My dear master," replied Cacambo, "Cunegonde is washing dishes on the banks of Propontis [1] for a prince who pos-

1. **Propontis** Now the Sea of Marmora, above the Dardanelles.

sesses very few dishes; she is a slave in the house of a for-
30 mer sovereign named Ragotsky,[2] who receives in his refuge
three crowns a day from the Grand Turk; but what is even
more sad is that she has lost her beauty and has become horribly ugly."

"Ah! beautiful or ugly," said Candide, "I am a man of
honor and my duty is to love her always. But how can she
be reduced to so abject a condition with the five or six millions you carried off?"

"Ah!" said Cacambo, "did I not have to give two millions
to Señor Don Fernando d'Ibaraa y Figueora y Mascarenes
40 y Lampourdos y Souza, Governor of Buenos Ayres, for permission to bring away Mademoiselle Cunegonde? And did
not a pirate bravely strip us of all the rest? And did not this
pirate take us to Cape Matapan, to Milo, to Nicaria, to
Samos, to Petra, to the Dardanelles, to Marmora, to Scutari?
Cunegonde and the old woman are servants to the prince I
mentioned, and I am slave to the dethroned Sultan."

"What a chain of terrible calamities!" said Candide. "But
after all, I still have a few diamonds; I shall easily deliver
Cunegonde. What a pity she has become so ugly."

50   Then, turning to Martin, he said: "Who do you think is
the most to be pitied, the Sultan Achmet, the Emperor Ivan,
King Charles Edward, or me?"

"I do not know at all," said Martin. "I should have to be
in your hearts to know."

"Ah!" said Candide, "if Pangloss were here he would
know and would tell us."

"I do not know," said Martin, "what scales your Pangloss
would use to weigh the misfortunes of men and to estimate
their sufferings. All I presume is that there are millions of
60 men on the earth a hundred times more to be pitied than
King Charles Edward, the Emperor Ivan and the Sultan
Achmet."

"That may very well be," said Candide.

In a few days they reached the Black Sea channel. Candide began by paying a high ransom for Cacambo and,

2. **Ragotsky** Formerly, Prince of Transylvania.

without wasting time, he went on board a galley with his companions bound for the shores of Propontis, in order to find Cunegonde however ugly she might be. Among the galley slaves were two convicts who rowed very badly and from time to time the Levantine captain applied several 70 strokes of a bull's pizzle to their naked shoulders. From a natural feeling of pity Candide watched them more attentively than the other galley slaves and went up to them. Some features of their disfigured faces appeared to him to have some resemblance to Pangloss and the wretched Jesuit, the Baron, Mademoiselle Cunegonde's brother. This idea disturbed and saddened him. He looked at them still more carefully. "Truly," said he to Cacambo, "if I had not seen Dr. Pangloss hanged, and if I had not been so unfortunate as to kill the Baron, I should think they were rowing in 80 this galley."

At the words Baron and Pangloss, the two convicts gave a loud cry, stopped on their seats and dropped their oars. The Levantine captain ran up to them and the lashes with the bull's pizzle were redoubled.

"Stop! Stop, sir!" cried Candide. "I will give you as much money as you want."

"What! Is it Candide?" said one of the convicts.

"What! Is it Candide?" said the other.

"Is it a dream?" said Candide. "Am I awake? Am I in 90 this galley? Is that my Lord the Baron whom I killed? Is that Dr. Pangloss whom I saw hanged?"

"It is, it is," they replied.

"What! Is that the great philosopher?" said Martin.

"Ah! sir," said Candide to the Levantine captain, "how much money do you want for My Lord Thunder-ten-tronckh, one of the first Barons of the empire, and for Dr. Pangloss, the most profound metaphysician of Germany?"

"Dog of a Christian," replied the Levantine captain, "since these two dogs of Christian convicts are Barons and 100 metaphysicians, which no doubt is a high rank in their country, you shall pay me fifty thousand sequins."

"You shall have them, sir. Row back to Constantinople

like lightning and you shall be paid at once. But, no, take me to Mademoiselle Cunegonde."

The captain, at Candide's first offer had already turned the bow towards the town, and rowed there more swiftly than a bird cleaves the air.

Candide embraced the Baron and Pangloss a hundred
110 times. "How was it I did not kill you, my dear Baron? And, my dear Pangloss, how do you happen to be alive after having been hanged? And why are you both in a Turkish galley?"

"Is it really true that my dear sister is in this country?" said the Baron.

"Yes," replied Cacambo.

"So once more I see my dear Candide!" cried Pangloss.

Candide introduced Martin and Cacambo. They all embraced and all talked at the same time. The galley flew; al-
120 ready they were in the harbor. They sent for a Jew, and Candide sold him for fifty thousand sequins a diamond worth a hundred thousand, for which he swore by Abraham he could not give any more. The ransom of the Baron and Pangloss was immediately paid. Pangloss threw himself at the feet of his liberator and bathed them with tears; the other thanked him with a nod and promised to repay the money at the first opportunity. "But is it possible that my sister is in Turkey?" said he.

"Nothing is so possible," replied Cacambo, "since she
130 washes up the dishes of a prince of Transylvania."

They immediately sent for two Jews; Candide sold some more diamonds; and they all set out in another galley to rescue Cunegonde.

Chapter XXVIII

WHAT HAPPENED TO CANDIDE, TO CUNEGONDE, TO PANGLOSS, TO MARTIN, ETC.

"Pardon once more," said Candide to the Baron, "pardon me, reverend father, for having thrust my sword through your body."

"Let us say no more about it," said the Baron. "I admit I was a little too sharp; but since you wish to know how it was you saw me in a galley, I must tell you that after my wound was healed by the brother apothecary of the college, I was attacked and carried off by a Spanish raiding party; I was imprisoned in Buenos Ayres at the time when my sister had just left. I asked to return to the Vicar-General in Rome. I was ordered to Constantinople to act as almoner to the Ambassador of France. A week after I had taken up my office I met towards evening a very handsome young page of the Sultan. It was very hot; the young man wished to bathe; I took the opportunity to bathe also. I did not know that it was a most serious crime for a Christian to be found naked with a young Mahometan. A cadi sentenced me to a hundred strokes on the soles of my feet and condemned me to the galley. I do not think a more horrible injustice has ever been committed. But I should very much like to know why my sister is in the kitchen of a Transylvanian sovereign living in exile among the Turks."

"But, my dear Pangloss," said Candide, "how does it happen that I see you once more?"

"It is true," said Pangloss, "that you saw me hanged: and in the natural course of events I should have been burned.[1]

1. **burned** But burning would not have served Voltaire's purposes.

105

But you remember, it poured with rain when they were going to roast me; the storm was so violent that they despaired
of lighting the fire; I was hanged because they could do noth-
30 ing better; a surgeon bought my body, carried me home and
dissected me. He first made a crucial incision in me from
the navel to the collarbone. Nobody could have been worse
hanged than I was. The executioner of the holy Inquisition,
who was a sub-deacon, was marvellously skilful in burning
people, but he was not accustomed to hang them; the rope
was wet and did not slide easily and it was knotted; in
short, I still breathed. The crucial incision caused me to
utter so loud a scream that the surgeon fell over backwards
and, thinking he was dissecting the devil, fled away in ter-
40 ror and fell down the staircase in his flight. His wife ran in
from another room at the noise; she saw me stretched out
on the table with my crucial incision; she was still more
frightened than her husband, fled, and fell on top of him.
When they had recovered themselves a little, I heard the
surgeon's wife say to the surgeon: 'My dear, what were you
thinking of, to dissect a heretic? Don't you know the devil
always possesses them? I will go and get a priest at once to
exorcise him.'

    "At this I shuddered and collected the little strength I
50 had left to shout: 'Have pity on me!' At last the Portuguese
barber [2] grew bolder; he sewed up my skin; his wife even
took care of me, and at the end of a fortnight I was able to
walk again. The barber found me a situation and made me
lackey to a Knight of Malta who was going to Venice; but,
as my master had no money to pay me wages, I entered the
service of a Venetian merchant and followed him to Constantinople.

    "One day I took it into my head to enter a mosque; there
was nobody there except an old Imam and a very pretty
60 young devotee who was reciting her prayers; her breasts
were entirely uncovered; between them she wore a bunch
of tulips, roses, anemones, ranunculus, hyacinths and auricu-
las; she dropped her bunch of flowers; I picked it up and

    2. barber Like the Barber of Seville, he was also the surgeon.

returned it to her with a most respectful alacrity. I was so long putting them back that the Imam grew angry and, seeing I was a Christian, called for help. I was taken to the cadi, who sentenced me to receive a hundred strokes on the soles of my feet and sent me to the galleys. I was chained on the same seat and in the same galley as My Lord the Baron. In this galley there were four young men from Marseilles, five Neapolitan priests and two monks from Corfu, who assured us that similar accidents occurred every day. His Lordship the Baron claimed that he had suffered a greater injustice than I; and I claimed that it was much more permissible to replace a bunch of flowers between a woman's breasts than to be naked with one of the Sultan's pages. We argued continually, and every day received twenty strokes of the bull's pizzle, when the chain of events of this universe led you to our galley and you ransomed us."

"Well! my dear Pangloss," said Candide, "when you were hanged, dissected, stunned with blows and made to row in the galleys, did you always think that everything was for the best in this world?"

"I am still of my first opinion," replied Pangloss, "for after all I am a philosopher; and it would be unbecoming for me to recant, since Leibnitz could not be in the wrong and pre-established harmony is the finest thing imaginable like the plenum and subtle matter." [3]

3. **matter** According to Leibnitz, harmony between the spiritual and material worlds was pre-established by God. The plenum and subtle matter form part of the German philosopher's outmoded physics.

Chapter XXIX

HOW CANDIDE FOUND CUNEGONDE AND THE OLD WOMAN AGAIN

While Candide, the Baron, Pangloss, Martin and Cacambo were relating their adventures, reasoning upon contingent [1] or non-contingent events of the universe, arguing about effects and causes, moral and physical evil, free will and necessity, and the consolation to be found in the Turkish galleys, they came to the house of the Transylvanian prince on the shores of Propontis.

The first objects which met their sight were Cunegonde and the old woman hanging out towels to dry on the line.

10 At this sight the Baron grew pale. Candide, that tender lover, seeing his fair Cunegonde sunburned, blear-eyed, flat-breasted, with wrinkles round her eyes and red, chapped arms, recoiled three paces in horror, and then advanced from mere politeness. She embraced Candide and her brother. They embraced the old woman; Candide bought them both.

In the neighborhood was a little farm; the old woman suggested that Candide should buy it, until some better fate befell the group. Cunegonde did not know that she had

20 become ugly, for nobody had told her so; she reminded Candide of his promises in so peremptory a tone that the good Candide dared not refuse her. He therefore informed the Baron that he was about to marry his sister.

"Never," said the Baron, "will I endure such baseness on her part and such insolence on yours; nobody shall ever reproach me with this infamy; my sister's children could

---

1. contingent A contingent event is a possible but not inevitable eventuality.

never enter the chapters [2] of Germany. No, my sister shall never marry anyone but a Baron of the Empire."

Cunegonde threw herself at his feet and bathed them in tears; but he was inflexible.

30

"Madman," said Candide, "I rescued you from the galleys, I paid your ransom and your sister's; she was washing dishes here, she is ugly, I am so kind as to make her my wife, and you pretend to oppose me! I should re-kill you if I listened to my anger."

"You may kill me again," said the Baron, "but you shall never marry my sister while I am alive."

2. **chapters** Knightly assemblies.

Chapter XXX

CONCLUSION

At the bottom of his heart Candide had not the least wish to marry Cunegonde. But the Baron's extreme impertinence determined him to complete the marriage, and Cunegonde urged it so warmly that he could not retract. He consulted Pangloss, Martin and the faithful Cacambo. Pangloss wrote an excellent memorandum by which he proved that the Baron had no rights over his sister and that by all the laws of the empire she could make a left-handed marriage [1] with Candide. Martin advised that the Baron should be thrown into the sea; Cacambo decided that he should be returned to the Levantine captain and sent back to the galleys, after which he would be returned by the first ship to the Vicar-General at Rome. This was thought to be very good advice; the old woman approved it; they said nothing to the sister; the plan was carried out with the aid of a little money and they had the pleasure of duping a Jesuit and punishing the pride of a German Baron.

It would be natural to suppose that when, after so many disasters, Candide was married to his mistress, and living with the philosopher Pangloss, the philosopher Martin, the prudent Cacambo and the old woman, having brought back so many diamonds from the country of the ancient Incas, he would lead the most pleasant life imaginable.[2] But he was so cheated by the Jews [3] that he had nothing left but his

1. **marriage** A morganatic marriage, which does not give equality to the party of lower rank.

2. **imaginable** If this were an idle tale of adventure, the couple would have been left here, to "live happily ever afterwards."

3. **Jews** Voltaire suffered several severe financial losses through the bankruptcies of Jewish bankers.

little farm; his wife, growing uglier every day, became
shrewish and unendurable; the old woman was ailing and
even more bad tempered than Cunegonde. Cacambo, who
worked in the garden and then went to Constantinople to
sell vegetables, was overworked and cursed his fate. Pangloss was in despair because he did not shine in some Ger- 30
man university.

As for Martin, he was firmly convinced that people are
equally uncomfortable everywhere; he accepted things patiently. Candide, Martin and Pangloss sometimes argued
about metaphysics and morals. From the windows of the
farm they often watched the ships going by, filled with effendis, pashas, and cadis, who were being exiled to Lemnos,
to Mitylene and Erzerum. They saw other cadis, other
pashas and other effendis coming back to take the place of
the exiles and to be exiled in their turn. They saw the neatly 40
impaled heads which were taken to the Sublime Porte.[4]
These sights redoubled their discussions; and when they
were not arguing, the boredom was so excessive that one
day the old woman dared to say to them: "I should like to
know which is worse, to be raped a hundred times by negro
pirates, to have a buttock cut off, to run the gauntlet among
the Bulgarians, to be whipped and flogged in an *auto-da-fé*,
to be dissected, to row in a galley, in short, to endure all the
miseries through which we have passed, or to remain here
doing nothing?" 50

" 'Tis a great question," said Candide.

These remarks led to new reflections, and Martin especially concluded that man was born to live in the convulsions of distress or in the lethargy of boredom. Candide did
not agree, but he asserted nothing. Pangloss confessed that
he had always suffered horribly; but, having once main-
tained that everything was for the best, he had continued
to maintain it without believing it.

One thing confirmed Martin in his destestable principles,
made Candide hesitate more than ever, and embarrassed 60

4. **Porte** The Gate of the Turkish Sultan's palace, which was also
the Palace of Justice.

Pangloss. And it was this. One day there came to their farm Paquette and Friar Giroflée, who were in the most extreme misery; they had soon wasted their three thousand piastres, had left each other, made it up, quarrelled again, been put in prison, escaped, and finally Friar Giroflée had turned Turk. Paquette continued her occupation everywhere and now earned nothing by it.

"I foresaw," said Martin to Candide, "that your gifts would soon be wasted and would only make them the more 70 miserable. You and Cacambo were once bloated with millions of piastres and you are no happier than Friar Giroflée and Paquette."

"Ah! Ha!" said Pangloss to Paquette, "so Heaven brings you back to us, my dear child? Do you know that you cost me the end of my nose, an eye and an ear! What a plight you are in! Ah! What a world this is!"

This new occurrence caused them to philosophise more than ever. In the neighborhood there lived a very famous Dervish, who was supposed to be the best philosopher in 80 Turkey; they went to consult him; Pangloss was the spokesman and said: "Master, we have come to beg you to tell us why so strange an animal as man was ever created."

"What has it to do with you?" said the Dervish. "Is it your business?"

"But, reverend father," said Candide, "there is a horrible amount of evil in the world."

"What does it matter," said the Dervish, "whether there is evil or good? When his highness sends a ship to Egypt, does he worry about the comfort or discomfort of the rats 90 in the ship?" [5]

"Then what should we do?" said Pangloss.

"Hold your tongue," said the Dervish.

"I flattered myself," said Pangloss, "that I should discuss with you effects and causes, this best of all possible worlds, the origin of evil, the nature of the soul and pre-established harmony."

5. **ship** This pessimistic passage seems to limit severely the extent of Divine Providence. Compare the ending of the Book of Job.

At these words the Dervish slammed the door in their faces.

During this conversation the news went round that at Constantinople two viziers and the mufti had been strangled and several of their friends impaled. This catastrophe made a prodigious noise everywhere for several hours. As Pangloss, Candide and Martin were returning to their little farm, they came upon an old man who was taking the air under a bower of orange trees at his door. Pangloss, who was as curious as he was argumentative, asked him what was the name of the mufti who had just been strangled.

"I do not know," replied the old man. "I have never known the name of any mufti or of any vizier. I am entirely ignorant of the occurrence you mention; I presume that in general those who meddle with public affairs sometimes perish miserably and that they deserve it; but I never inquire what is going on in Constantinople; I content myself with sending there for sale the produce of the garden I cultivate."

Having spoken thus, he took the strangers into his house. His two daughters and his two sons presented them with several kinds of sherbert which they made themselves, caymac flavored with candied citron peel, oranges, lemons, limes, pineapples, dates, pistachios and Mocha coffee which had not been mixed with the bad coffee of Batavia and the Isles. After which this good Mussulman's two daughters perfumed the beards of Candide, Pangloss and Martin.

"You must have a vast and magnificent estate?" said Candide to the Turk.

"I have only twenty acres," replied the Turk. "I cultivate them with my children; and work keeps at bay three great evils: boredom, vice and need." [6]

As Candide returned to his farm he reflected deeply on the Turk's remarks. He said to Pangloss and Martin: "That good old man seems to me to have chosen an existence pref-

6. **need** This is the key to Voltaire's philosophy of life. *Candide* gives abundant examples of all three of these evils.

erable by far to that of the six kings with whom we had the honor to sup."

"Exalted rank," said Pangloss, "is very dangerous, according to the testimony of all philosophers; for Eglon, King of the Moabites, was murdered by Ehud; Absalom was hanged by the hair and pierced by three darts; King Nadab, son of Jeroboam, was killed by Baasha; King Elah by Zimri; Ahaziah by Jehu; Athaliah by Jehoiada; the Kings Jehoi-
140 akim, Jeconiah and Zedekiah were made slaves.[7] You know in what manner died Crœsus, Astyages, Darius, Denys of Syracuse, Pyrrhus, Perseus, Hannibal, Jugurtha, Ariovistus, Cæsar, Pompey, Nero, Otho, Vitellius, Domitian, Richard ii of England, Edward ii, Henry vi, Richard iii, Mary Stuart, Charles i, the three Henrys of France, the Emperor Henry iv. You know . . ."

"I also know," said Candide, "that we should cultivate our gardens."

"You are right," said Pangloss, "for, when man was
150 placed in the Garden of Eden, he was placed there *ut operaretur eum,* to dress it and to keep it; which proves that man was not born for idleness."

"Let us work without theorizing," [8] said Martin; " 'tis the only way to make life endurable."

The whole small fraternity entered into this praiseworthy plan, and each started to make use of his talents. The little farm yielded well. Cunegonde was indeed very ugly, but she became an excellent pastry cook; Paquette embroidered; the old woman took care of the linen. Even Friar Giroflée
160 performed some service; he was a very good carpenter and even became a man of honor; and Pangloss sometimes said to Candide: "All events are linked up in this best of all possible worlds; for, if you had not been expelled from the noble castle, by hard kicks in your backside for love of

7. **slaves** To explain these Biblical references would be pedantry— which Voltaire is here satirizing.

8. **theorizing** I.e., since men can never grasp the ultimate ends of life, let us make the best of it without worrying—an "optimistic" acceptance of life as it is.

Mademoiselle Cunegonde, if you had not been clapped into the Inquisition, if you had not wandered about America on foot, if you had not stuck your sword in the Baron, if you had not lost all your sheep from the land of Eldorado, you would not be eating candied citrons and pistachios here." [9]

" 'Tis well said," replied Candide, "but we must culti- 170 vate our gardens."

9. **here** The final reduction of Pangloss's philosophy to the absurd.

Bibliography

Voltaire, *Candide, ou l'optimisme*. Edition critique avec une introduction et un commentaire, par André Morize. Paris, Hachette, 1913.

G. Brandes, *Voltaire* (Biography in English translation), New York, Tudor, n. d.

S. G. Tallentyre, *The Life of Voltaire*, London, Smith, Elder, 1903.

Arthur O. Lovejoy, *The Great Chain of Being*. Cambridge (Mass.), Harvard University Press, 1936. (Ch. VII—"Eighteenth-Century Optimism.")

John Morley, *Voltaire*, London, 1874.

James Parton, *Life of Voltaire*, Boston, 1881, 2 vols.

Alfred Noyes, *Voltaire*, New York, Sheed & Ward, 1936.

Norman L. Torrey, *The Spirit of Voltaire*, Oxford (England), The Marston Press, 1963.